内 閣 総 理 大 臣 へ の 道
The Road to the Top

装幀・
カバーイラスト＝斉藤　啓

本文イラスト＝テッド高橋
※本文中のイラスト・図版は、対訳ニッポン双書『全図解 日本のしくみ』（弊社刊）より転載しています。

BILINGUAL BOOKS FOR BEGINNERS

内閣総理大臣への道
The Road to the Top

著＝深山 真
訳＝クリストファー・ベルトン

Foreword

How can one rise to become the top leader of Japan?

The Constitution does not clarify who is able to reach the top. The Emperor is recognized as the symbol of the unity of the people, so it could be said that the Emperor is the leader of Japan. However, the Emperor's role is hereditary, and it is not a position to which average citizens are able to aspire.

In which case, what it the highest position to which average citizens may aspire? Japan's Constitution stipulates a system known as the separation of powers (into three powers; administration, legislation, and judicature). In other words, three people wield the nation's topmost levels of power.

The three most powerful people in Japan are the Prime Minister, the Speaker of the House of Representatives (the Diet is divided into two Houses, with the House of Representatives taking precedence over the House of Councillors), and the Chief Justice of the Supreme Court. How did these three people get appointed to their positions?

The people aspiring to reach the summit of politics first of all align their sights with becoming the Prime Minister. It goes without saying that many paths lead to this position. Here we will examine the road to the position of Prime Minister from the peripherals of regional politics.

はじめに

　日本ではどうやったら国のトップになれるのでしょうか？

　日本国憲法では明確に国のトップが誰かを定めていません。天皇は国民統合の象徴と定められていますので、一応トップと言って良いでしょう。ただ、天皇は世襲ですから、一般の人がなれる地位ではありません。

　では一般の人がなれる国の最高の地位は何でしょうか？　日本国憲法では、三権分立という制度を定めています。よって、国の最高権力者は3人いることになります。

　内閣総理大臣、衆議院議長（国会は二院制ですが、参議院より衆議院が優越しています）、最高裁判所長官、これが日本の最高権力者です。ではその地位にはどうしたら就けるのでしょうか？

　まずは政府のトップ、内閣総理大臣を目指します。もちろんトップに至る道は様々です。ここでは地方からの順を追って内閣総理大臣になる道を考えて行きます。

目次

Foreword 4
はじめに

| Chapter 1 | **Regional Politics** 11
第1章　地方の政治

1. **Civic Activities** 12
   市民活動

   [1] Aspiring to Politics　政治を志す...... 12
   [2] Making a Move　具体的に動く...... 14
   [3] Standing for the City Assembly　市議会に立候補する...... 16
   [4] Election Activities　選挙活動...... 18

2. **City Assemblies** 21
   市議会

   [1] Ward, City, Town and Village Assemblies
       区市町村議会とは...... 21
   [2] Deciding on a Faction　会派を決める...... 24
   [3] Assembly Member Activities　議員活動...... 26

3. **Mayors** 29
   市長

   [1] Standing for Mayor　市長選に立候補する...... 29
   [2] Having been Elected Mayor　市長当選後...... 32
   [3] Main Issues Facing Today's Municipalities
       現代の基礎自治体の主な課題...... 34

4 Prefectural Administration 36
都道府県政

- [1] Standing for the Prefectural Assembly
  都道府県議会への立候補 36
- [2] Role of Members of the Prefectural Assembly
  都道府県議会議員の役割 39
- [3] Becoming Prefectural Governor 知事になる 41
- [4] Job of the Prefectural Governor 知事の仕事 43
- [5] Main Issues Facing Today's Prefectural Administration
  都道府県政の課題 46

Chapter 2 National Diet Members 49
第 2 章　国会議員

1 Becoming a Member of the National Diet 50
国会議員になる

- [1] What are Diet Members? 国会議員とは 50
- [2] Standing for the National Diet 国会議員に出馬 53

2 Political Parties 56
政党

- [1] History of Japan's Political Parties 日本の政党の歴史 56
- [2] The Liberal Democratic Party 自由民主党 59
- [3] The Democratic Party of Japan 民主党 62
- [4] Other Political Parties その他の政党 64

3 Elections 66
   選挙
   [1] House of Representatives Election 衆議院議員選挙 66
   [2] House of Councillors Election 参議院議員選挙 69

4 The House 72
   議院
   [1] The Job of Diet Members 国会議員の仕事 72
   [2] Resolving Matters in the Diet 国会の決議方法 75
   [3] The House of Representatives 衆議院 78
   [4] The House of Councillors 参議院 81

Chapter 3 The Government 85
第3章　政府

1 The Prime Minister 86
   内閣総理大臣
   [1] Becoming the Prime Minister 内閣総理大臣になる 86
   [2] What is the Cabinet? 内閣とは 89
   [3] The Job of the Prime Minister 内閣総理大臣の仕事 92

2 Ministers of State 94
   国務大臣
   [1] Japan's Ministries, Bureaus and Agencies
       日本の省庁 94
   [2] The Job of Ministers of State 国務大臣の仕事 97

3 Modern Political Issues (Domestic Issues) 99
現代の政治課題（内政）

- [1] Revising the Constitution 憲法改正問題 99
- [2] Recovery in the Aftermath of the Great Eastern Japan Earthquake 東日本大震災復興問題 101
- [3] Economic Recovery 景気回復問題 104
- [4] Financial Reform 財政再建問題 106
- [5] Energy エネルギー問題 109
- [6] Administrative Reform 行政改革問題 112
- [7] Public Works 公共事業問題 115
- [8] Social Welfare 社会福祉問題 117
- [9] Educational Reform 教育改革問題 119
- [10] Electoral System 選挙制度問題 122
- [11] TPP TPP問題 124
- [12] Territorial Rights 領土問題 126
- [13] Abductions 拉致問題 129
- [14] Military Bases 基地問題 131

Chapter 4 Diplomacy 135
第4章　外交

1 The Mechanisms of Diplomacy 136
外交のしくみ

- [1] Diplomats 外交官 136
- [2] The United Nations 国連 139
- [3] Summits and other International Conferences サミットなどの国際会議 142

2 Japan's Diplomatic Issues 144
日本の外交問題

- [1] Japan and America 日米問題 144
- [2] Japan and China 日中問題 147
- [3] Japan and South Korea #1 日韓問題1 150
- [4] Japan and South Korea #2 日韓問題2 152
- [5] Japan and Russia 日露問題 155
- [6] Diplomacy in Asia アジア地域との外交 158
- [7] Diplomacy in the Middle East 中東地域との外交 160
- [8] Diplomacy in Africa アフリカ地域との外交 162
- [9] Diplomacy in Europe ヨーロッパ地域との外交 164

Appendix Japan's Judicial System 167
付録　日本の裁判制度

1 Judicial Independence 168
司法権の独立

2 Three-Tier Appeal System 170
三審制

3 Becoming a Judge 172
裁判官になる方法

4 Judicial System Reforms 174
司法制度改革

Chapter 1
Regional Politics

▶▶▶▶▶▶▶

第1章　地方の政治

1 Civic Activities
市民活動

[1] Aspiring to Politics

① What motives do people who aspire to become politicians have? There are sure to be some aspiring politicians who are motivated by a desire for power, glory and financial reward. There are also probably those who had politicians in their families and wish to carry on the tradition. However, without an immense amount of dedication, it is impossible to carry out the never-ending activities of a politician armed simply with this level of motivation.

② The reason for this is because politicians have to be elected in elections. People who only enter politics for their own sakes will be viewed as power-grabbers and will get very little public support.

③ Owing to this, and with the exception of a few well-known people, it is extremely important for politicians to be active in their local areas on a daily basis. It is necessary for them to get involved in social activities that are driven by such ambitions as, for example, changing the current education system, stimulating the economic growth of the town, or changing the social system for disabled people and other people on a weak footing.

④ It is activities like this that represent the first step that average people aspiring to politics must take, and it has nothing to do with being famous or being born into a family of bureaucrats or politicians.

▶▶▶▶▶▶

[1] 政治を志す

❶ 政治家を目指す人はどういう動機を持っているのでしょうか？ 個人的な権力欲、名誉欲、そして金儲けといった動機で政治家を志す人もいるでしょう。さらに政治家の家庭に生まれたので、そのまま後を継いだという人もいるでしょう。しかし、よほどのことがない限り、それだけの理由では、なかなか息の長い政治家生活は送れません。

❷ なぜなら、政治家は必ず選挙で選ばれなくてはならないからです。この人ならば自分たちのために政治をしてくれると有権者に思わせ、支持を得なければなりません。

❸ そのためには、一部の有名人をのぞいて、日常的な地元での活動が重要です。例えば、現在の教育を変えたい、町の経済を発展させたい、障害のある人など弱い人の立場で社会制度を変えたいなどの志を基に、社会的な活動をしていくことが必要なのです。

❹ 有名人でもなく、官僚でも、政治家の家に生まれたわけでもない一般の人が政治家になる第一歩が、こうした活動と言えるでしょう。

[2] Making a Move

① Unknown people who wish to become politicians must start off their careers by doing something worthwhile. There are sure to be many activities that one can involve oneself in the area one lives, such as revitalizing the local shopping district, helping the homeless or volunteering one's services during emergencies.

② Issues that affect governmental policies on a national scale, such as education and military bases, etc., also provide targets for activities. Becoming involved in neighborhood assemblies and helping out during local festivals could also be said to be the first step on the road to becoming a politician. Joining the staff of a local politician whose beliefs coincide with one's own as a secretary would also represent a large step to success.

③ The freedom of political activity is guaranteed in Japan. The freedom of speech, the freedom of assembly and the freedom of association are also basic rights that are protected by the Constitution. Making the best use of these rights to gather people of the same mind together and act as their leader is the first and most important step in becoming a politician.

[2] 具体的に動く

❶ もし無名な人が政治家になりたければ、自分でなにか具体的に動くことから始めなくてはなりません。商店街の活性化やホームレスの救済、災害時のボランティアなど、自分が住んでいる地域に関わる問題を中心に活動することもあるでしょう。

❷ また、国全体の政策に関わる問題、例えば教育の充実や基地問題なども活動の現場になります。地域の自治会の役員や、祭りの世話役になることなども政治家への第一歩と言えます。自分の理想に近い政治家の事務所に入り、秘書として活動することも大きなステップと言えます。

❸ 日本は政治活動の自由が保障されています。言論、集会、結社の自由も憲法で保障された基本的な権利です。こうした権利を行使し、賛同する人を集め、そこでリーダーシップをとっていくことこそが、最初の、そして最も重要な政治家への第一歩となるでしょう。

[3] Standing for the City Assembly

① Having worked hard in local activities and built up a large number of supporters, the next step to becoming a politician is to stand for a seat on the neighborhood assembly. The special wards of Tokyo (23 wards), cities, towns and villages are known as municipalities.

② Municipalities represent the smallest unit of national administration, and assembly members and mayors of these units are elected directly by local citizens over the age of 20 in Japan. It is also possible to stand as a candidate having reached the age of 25 or older.

③ People elected to the assembly of a municipality are bona fide politicians. It is necessary to pay a deposit to the regional Legal Affairs Bureau in order to become a candidate for a seat on the assembly. This system is designed to prevent excessive numbers of candidates running for a limited number of seats, and a sum of ¥300,000 is required as a deposit to run for a city assembly. This deposit is returned in the event of the candidate being elected or receiving more than a predetermined number of votes, but it is confiscated in all other events. Deposits are not required when standing for town or village assemblies.

④ Having paid the deposit in order to stand in an election, it is then necessary to submit a declaration of intention to run as a candidate to the Election Administration Committee. The conditions that govern standing for election are; the candidate must be a Japanese national; he/she must have lived within the relevant municipality for three or more months; his/her civil rights must not have been curtailed as a result of committing a crime or any other reason.

▶▶▶▶▶▶

[3] 市議会に立候補する

❶ 地域での活動に力を注ぎ、多くの賛同者を得たなら、次は地元自治体の議会に立候補することが政治家への次のステップとなります。東京の特別区（東京23区）、市町村のことを基礎自治体と言います。

❷ 基礎自治体は、国の行政区画の中で最小の単位で、日本では20歳以上の住民による直接選挙によって議会議員と首長（村長や市長など）を選びます。また、25歳以上になるとそれに立候補することができます。

❸ 基礎自治体の議員になったならば、もう立派な政治家です。立候補するためには法務局に供託金を納めなくてはなりません。これは立候補者の乱立を避けるための制度で、市議会議員なら30万円が必要です。当選、もしくは一定以上の結果を残した場合は、供託金は返還されますが、それ以外は没収されます。町村議会には供託金は必要ありません。

❹ 選挙に立候補する場合、この供託金を納めた上で、選挙管理委員会で立候補の届け出をします。また立候補するためには日本国籍を持っていること、その自治体に3ヵ月以上住んでいること、犯罪等により公民権が停止されていないことが条件になります。

[4] Election Activities

① Election activities begin once all of the candidacy procedures have been completed. The term of office for members of municipal assemblies is four years, and it is necessary to notify the electorate in detail of the plans the candidate intends to carry out during this term. This has become to be known as a "manifest" in recent years, but in simpler terms it is a list of election promises.

② During the election period, the candidate explains his/her promises to as many voters as possible and appeals for support. As this is not easily done alone, the candidate opens an election office and gathers together a team of supporters.

③ Although one method of gaining support is to be recommended by a political party whose beliefs are close to the person running for election, many of the candidates run for a seat on municipal assemblies as non-partisan candidates.

④ Election activities that can be commonly seen include

candidates driving around the streets in election cars giving speeches and repeatedly calling out their names. All elections are controlled by the Election Administration Committee in accordance with stipulations laid down in the Public Office Election Law. It is illegal to carry out election activities that are in violation of this, such as purchasing votes, even unintentionally.

▶▶▶▶▶

[4] 選挙活動
❶ 立候補の手続きがすんだら選挙活動を行います。基礎自治体の議員の任期は4年ですから、その間に何をしていくのかを具体的にまとめ、有権者に公表します。近年これをマニフェストと呼んでいますが、簡単に言えば選挙公約です。
❷ 立候補者は、選挙期間中、これを有権者に広く訴えていきます。一人で訴えることは難しいので、選挙事務所を設け、応援してくれる人を集めます。
❸ 自分の理想に近い政党の推薦を受けることも一つの方法ですが、基礎自治体議会の場合、多くの立候補者は無所属で闘っています。
❹ 選挙運動としては、選挙カーでの街頭演説や名前の連呼がよく見受けられます。こうした選挙は全て公職選挙法の規定により選挙管理委員会が管理します。間違っても買収などの選挙違反をしてはいけません。

⑤ It is said that running for election in Japan is a very expensive business. Sometimes there are cases in which vote-purchasing is detected, but candidates are subject to arrest if accused of this and their political life will come to an end if they are found guilty. Only clean election activities will be tolerated.

▶▶▶▶▶▶

[4] 選挙活動 つづき

❺ 日本の選挙はお金がかかると言われています。一部には買収等の事実を指摘される場合がありますが、もし発覚すれば逮捕され、有罪になると政治生命も奪われます。クリーンな選挙が広く求められています。

2 City Assemblies
市議会

[1] Ward, City, Town and Village Assemblies

① Candidates elected to a seat on an assembly are now politicians.

② The method of running assemblies is the same for the special wards in Tokyo and in cities, towns and villages. Every member of the assembly has been duly elected to the position through the electoral procedure. The term of office is four years, and during this period the members of the assembly will be involved in proposing, debating and approving the municipal budget.

③ They may also submit memorandums to the national and prefectural administrations and pledge to have local opinion represented in policies. They are also able to investigate all activities undertaken within the municipality and demand rectification if necessary, as well as seek damages and file criminal charges.

④ Although the term of office lasts for four years, it is possible for assembly members to lose their jobs if the assembly is disbanded owing to a recall election initiated through a petition organized by the electorate. Members can also lose their jobs before their four-year term of office is complete in the event of a vote of no-confidence being passed against the chairman of the assembly, and in the event of four-fifths or more of the total number of assembly members agreeing to disband the assembly voluntarily.

⑤ Assembly meetings are split into regular sessions and extraordinary sessions, with the regular sessions usually being held four times per year. These sessions are also split into committee meetings and main meetings, although in the end the motions passed in the main meetings are the ones that are approved. Assembly members are paid from the municipality's budget. The chairman of the assembly

is elected by the assembly members and is responsible for overall administration.
　　　　　　　　　　　　　　　　　　　　　　　　　　～の責任を負う
全体の

[1] 区市町村議会とは

❶ 当選したら議会議員となり、政治家の一員となります。

❷ 東京の特別区も市町村も議会のあり方は同じです。議会議員は全員選挙で選ばれた人たちです。議会の任期は4年で、この間に、自治体の予算や条例を発議、審議、承認することがその仕事です。

❸ また、都道府県や国に対して意見書を提出し、地方の意見を反映させる誓願を行うこともできます。さらに自治体の活動全般を調査し、必要に応じて是正を求め、損害賠償や刑事告発を行うこともできます。

❹ 任期は4年ですが、住民のリコールで議会が解散した場合、失職することもあります。首長の不信任が可決した場合の首長による議会解散、議員数の5分の4以上の賛成による自主解散があった場合も、4年を経たずに解散し、失職することもあります。

❺ 会議には、定例会と臨時会があり、定例会は通常年間4回行われます。また、会議は委員会と本会議に分けられ、最終的には本会議の決定をもって議題は可決とされます。なお、議員の報酬は自治体の会計から支出されます。議長は議員から互選され議会の運営に責任を持ちます。

[2] Deciding on a Faction

① In many cases, assembly members join together into factions with other assembly members who have similar ways of thinking and similar ideals and carry out their activities based on the dictates of these factions. The amount of time that questions can be asked during assembly meetings is determined by the number of members each faction has.

② Although there are cases in which factions are centered on political parties, there are also cases in which local political parties and the Japanese Communist Party, etc., make their own municipal factions. However, very few candidates running for seats on the assembly are supported or officially approved by political parties—with most candidates running on independent tickets—and it is very rare to see factions overtly established by Japan's two current major parties; the Liberal Democratic Party and the Democratic Party of Japan. Many of the heads of municipalities also tend to be independents, so factions based on political party standards are not created in assemblies.

③ Under normal circumstances, the factions that are not affiliated to political parties are usually based on agreement or disagreement with the administrative policies of the head of the assembly. Having been elected to a seat on the assembly, the first thing to do is decide on which faction to join or whether to remain a lone wolf and not join any faction.

▶▶▶▶▶▶

[2] 会派を決める

❶ 議員としての活動は、多くの場合、考え方が近く、理想を共有する議員が集まって結成する会派を中心に行われます。議会では会派を構成する議員の数によって質問時間などが決められます。

❷ 会派は、政党を中心に集まる場合もありますが、地域政党や日本共産党などが基礎自治体の会派を作っているケースもあります。しかし、基礎自治体では、政党の支持や公認で立候補した議員は少なく、多くの議員が無所属なので、現在の日本の2大政党である自民党や民主党など政党が前面に出た会派を作っているケースはあまり見かけません。また、基礎自治体の首長も多くは無所属なので、議会でも政党基準での会派はあまり作られないのです。

❸ 政党とは別に会派を結成する場合、通常は、首長の施政方針に基本的に賛同するか否かが基準となります。議員になったら、最初にどこの会派に属すか、属さずに一匹狼の無所属を貫くかを決めなくてはなりません。

[3] Assembly Member Activities

① Assembly member activities finally begin once an affiliation has been established with a faction. Members cooperate with other members in the same faction to state their opinions during assembly meetings in order to realize the administrative policies to which they have committed themselves. The most important job for the assembly is to decide the budget for the municipality.

② The budget is a detailed estimation of the costs involved in implementing administrative policy, and it could be said that all administrative policies are tied into it. Because of this, it is necessary to have a clear understanding of the budget in order to make sure that all administrative polices that need to be implemented are covered within it.

③ The biggest issue that regional municipalities currently face is acquiring the finances for settling the budget. Tax revenues are not increasing and the financial assistance and subsidies received from the central government and

prefectures are being cut back. This means that it is
　　都道府県　　　　　　　　　　　削減されている
necessary to create new bylaws and modify the organization
　　　　　　　　　　　　　　　条例　　　　　　修正する　　組織
of the municipality in order to settle the budget.

[3] 議員活動

❶ 会派に属したら、いよいよ議員活動の開始です。思い抱いていた政策を実現するために、同じ会派の議員と協力して議会で発言します。議会で最も重要な仕事は、その自治体の予算を決めることです。

❷ 予算とは具体的な政策があって、それにかかる費用を見積もることですから、政策は全てこの予算に結集されていると言うことができます。ですから、政策を実現するためには、この予算を理解した上で、政策を反映させて行かなくてはなりません。

❸ 今、地方自治体が抱える重大な問題は、予算の財源の問題です。税収は伸びず、国や都道府県からの補助や交付金も削られています。これを解決するためには、新たな条例を作って自治体の仕組みを変えていくことも必要でしょう。

④ The activities of the assembly must also include providing feedback to voters at all times. In many cases this is achieved by assembly members holding local administrative policy briefing meetings and providing voters with information via leaflets and public postings. Members are also diligent in making appearances at neighborhood meetings and other gatherings, where they not only get the opportunity to explain the details of their own activities, but also get the chance to listen directly to the comments of voters so that they can reflect public opinion back into future activities; both of which are extremely important political activities.

▶▶▶▶▶▶

[3] 議員活動 つづき
❹ こうした議会での活動は、常に有権者にフィードバックする必要があります。多くの場合、議員は、市政報告会を地域で開催したり、チラシをポスティングしたりすることで有権者と連絡を取り合います。また地域の会合などにマメに顔を出し、活動内容を説明するとともに、有権者の声を直接聞いて次の活動に生かしていくことも重要な政治活動となります。

3 Mayors
市長

[1] Standing for Mayor

① Assembly members who have managed to accumulate results through their assembly activities can then accept the challenge of becoming the head of the assembly (the mayor in the case of cities). Although assembly members are able to work to achieve the administrative polices that are dear to them, their main job involves debating budget proposals and bylaw proposals submitted by the administration. The members that are dedicated to ensuring their own policies are enacted consequently need to attain the top position in the administration.

② In order to attain the administration's top position it is, of course, necessary to get elected. The election and candidate nomination procedures are basically the same as those for getting a seat on the assembly, but a deposit amounting to

¥1,000,000 is necessary to become a city mayor (¥500,000 for towns and villages, and ¥2,400,000 to become mayor of an ordinance-designated cities, which are normally recognized as big cities). It is also necessary to acquire ten percent of the minimum number of votes required by law.

③ Also, in mayoral elections there are cases in which independent candidates can receive the support or recommendation of political parties. This not only facilitates election, it also makes it easier to run the assembly after election.

④ This links municipal policy and each relevant political party together, and, it is necessary for the candidate to take the policies of each party into consideration. This is known as "*Kakuto Ainori*" (candidates supported by more than one party) in Japan, and although this system is criticized because it means that political parties that oppose each other on national policy are supporting the same candidate, it continues to be observed today.

[1] 市長選に立候補する

❶ 議員活動での実績が積み重なってきたら、次は首長（市の場合は市長）にチャレンジします。議会議員でも、自分の政策を実現するために動くことは可能ですが、行政が提出した予算案や条例案を審議することが主な仕事となります。独自の政策を実現しようとするのであれば、行政のトップにつくことです。

❷ 行政のトップになるためには、やはり選挙で当選しなければなりません。選挙や立候補の方法は、基本的には議会と同じですが、供託金が市の場合は100万円必要です（町村は50万円、大都市である政令指定都市は240万円）。また、法定得票数は有権者総数の10分の1となります。

❸ また市長選挙では、無所属の立候補でも、政党の支持か推薦を受ける場合があります。その方が当選しやすいだけでなく、当選後の議会運営もスムーズになるからです。

❹ その場合、各政党と政策協定を結び、それぞれの政党の政策にも配慮する必要があります。これを「各党相乗り」といい、国政では対立している政党が同じ人を押すこともあるため批判されることも多いですが、現実としてはそれが続いています。

[2] Having been Elected Mayor

① Once a candidate has been elected mayor, it means that he/she is the highest ranking person in the municipal administration. The first things they have to attend to after the election are to be briefed by the outgoing mayor in order to take over the job smoothly, and to receive lectures on all of the issues faced by the city administration. They also need to interact with voters and brush up on administrative policy.

② Having been appointed mayor, the vice-mayor and other members of the executive committee who will run the assembly are decided upon. The other people who represent the front line of battle at the city hall must also be appointed. Establishing a pipeline with the national and prefectural administrations is also an important task that the mayor must handle.

③ The most important daily job for a mayor is to compile the budget. With a few exceptions, settling finances is the most difficult job that municipalities face out of all the policies

mayors must implement alone in current-day Japan. They
need to establish close levels of communications with the
government and prefectural administration in order to solve
all financial problems. The most helpful factor in this is
establishing a network of contacts. It is no exaggeration to
say that the most important job that a mayor is faced with is
cultivating human relationships.

▶▶▶▶▶

[2] 市長当選後

❶ 市長に当選することは、その地域の行政の最高責任者になることになります。当選後には、まず前市長との行政の引き継ぎや市政の様々な問題点のレクチャーを受けることから始めます。また、有権者とさらに対話をして、政策をブラッシュアップしていく必要があります。

❷ 市長に就任すると、副市長などの執行部を決定し行政運営にあたります。また政策を実行するための布陣として役所の人事を決めます。国や都道府県とのパイプの構築なども、市長にとって重要な仕事です。

❸ 市長の日常的な業務として最も重要なのは、予算を編成することです。現在の日本では、基礎自治体が単独で政策を実施することは、一部の例外を除いて、財政的に非常に困難です。国や都道府県と連絡を密にして財政的な問題を解決していかなくてはなりません。そこで生きてくるのが人的なパイプ作りなのです。結局、こうした人脈の開拓が市長の一番重要な仕事といって過言はないでしょう。

[3] Main Issues Facing Today's Municipalities

① Cities, towns and villages are the frontline bases for championing the welfare of their citizens. In principle, municipalities are in charge of infant welfare, senior citizen welfare, mother and child support, support for the needy and other forms of support. Social welfare requires large sums of money, and securing the funds for this is an extremely important task.

② However, the long-term recession that followed on from the burst of the economic bubble severely suppressed the financial resources of municipalities. Public bonds were issued and financial resources were secured through loans to overcome this crisis, but loans have to be paid back. Paying off these loans currently accounts for a large proportion of municipal finances, which is a huge problem.

③ In order to return finances to a healthy state, it is necessary to raise tax revenue. However, simply increasing taxes places a heavier burden on local residents, which can result in

a negative economic effect.
マイナスの経済効果

④ Important administrative policies to counteract this include the establishment of initiatives to attract industry into the area, nurture local industry, develop tourist resources, revitalize shopping districts, as well as other such measures. It is said that the greatest administrative issue facing modern-day municipalities is the formulation of policies that will revitalize the local economy without lowering the standard of social welfare.

政策 / 対抗する / 〜を含む / 主導力の確立 / 企業の地元誘致 / 育成 / 地場産業 / 観光資源 / 〜を活性化する / 商店街 / 方策 / 今日の / 政策の立案 / 〜の水準 / 社会福祉

▶▶▶▶▶

[3] 現代の基礎自治体の主な課題

❶ 市町村は住民福祉の前線基地です。児童福祉、高齢者福祉、母子家庭支援、生活困窮者の支援などは基本的に基礎自治体が担っています。こうした福祉活動には大きな予算が必要であり、その財源を確保することが重要な仕事となります。

❷ しかし、バブル崩壊以降の長期的な不況のために、基礎自治体の財源は大きく落ち込んでいます。急場をしのぐために公債を発行し、借金で財源をまかなっていますが、借金は必ず返済しなくてはなりません。現在、この借金の返済が財政に大きくのしかかっているのが最大の問題です。

❸ 財政を健全化するためには税収を伸ばす必要があります。しかし、安易な増税は住民に大きな負担を強いることになるため、かえって経済的にはマイナスになる場合があります。

❹ そこで必要となる重要な政策は、企業誘致や地場産業の育成、観光資源の開発、商店街の活性化などへの取り組みです。福祉レベルを落とさずに、経済を活性化させる、これが現代の基礎自治体の一番大きな政策課題と言えます。

4 ▶ Prefectural Administration
都道府県政

[1] Standing for the Prefectural Assembly

① Having built up political muscle in municipal administration, the next step up the ladder is the prefectural assembly (a collective title that also includes the assemblies of Tokyo, Kyoto, Osaka and Hokkaido). In the same way as city assemblies, prefectural assemblies are re-elected once every four years. In addition to handling the political issues that are prevalent over a wide area that exceeds the jurisdiction of cities, towns and villages, prefectural assemblies must also provide indirect assistance for the individual administrative policies of all cities, towns and villages within its borders. Debating each of these policies is the job of the prefectural assembly.

② The conditions that govern standing for election are; the candidate must be a Japanese national; he/she must be

25 years of age or older and have lived within the relevant prefecture for three or more months; his/her civil rights must not have been curtailed as a result of committing a crime or any other reason. The required deposit is ¥600,000.

③ Contrary to assemblies in cities, towns and villages, prefectural assemblies have a more pronounced tendency toward political parties. This does not mean only the Liberal Democratic Party, the Democratic Party of Japan, New Komeito, the Communist Party, the Social Democratic Party and other parties involved in national politics, but also local political parties, such as the Tokyo Seikatsusha Network in Tokyo, the Osaka Restoration Association in Osaka, and the Shakai Taishuto in Okinawa.

④ Although it is possible to obtain a seat on these assemblies as an independent, in many cases political activities can be carried out more effectively if affiliated to a political party that shares similar sentiments, and deciding on which party to select is an extremely important decision that will

affect the candidate's future political career. It is common
　　　　～に影響を及ぼす　　　　　　　政治キャリア　　　　　　　　　～なのはよくあることだ
for factions affiliated to political parties to be created in
　　　会派　　　～と提携する　　　　　　　　　　　　　　結成される
prefectural assemblies and the assembly run accordingly.
　　　　　　　　　　　　　　　　　　　　　　　　　　　　それに応じて

▶▶▶▶▶▶

[1] 都道府県議会への立候補

❶ 市政で実力を蓄えたならば、次は県議会（東京都、京都府、大阪府、北海道も含む）です。県議会は市議会と同様に4年で改選があります。県は市町村の枠に収まらない広域の政治課題を扱うとともに、市町村の個別の政策の側面援助を行います。そうした政策を議論するのが県議会です。

❷ 県議会議員の被選挙権は、日本国籍を有し、25歳以上で3ヵ月以上その地域の住民であること、犯罪等で公民権が停止されていないことが必要です。供託金は60万円です。

❸ 市町村と違い、県議会になると議員に政党色が出てきます。自民党、民主党、公明党、共産党、社民党といった国政に関与する政党だけでなく、例えば東京都などは生活者ネットワーク、大阪府では先に国政にも進出した大阪維新の会、沖縄では社会大衆党などの地域政党もあります。

❹ 無所属も可能ですが、自分の政策に近い政党で活動することが効率的な政治活動になる場合が多く、どの政党を選ぶかが、政治家として今後に関わる重大な政治判断となります。都道府県議会では、多くの場合、政党を母体とした会派が結成され、議会の運営を行います。

[2] Role of Members of the Prefectural Assembly

① So, what is the role of prefectural assemblies? The main tasks for assembly members include debating policy, approving budgets, enacting bylaws and other chores; basically in the same way as the city, town and village assemblies. In addition to this, in most cases prefectural assembly members are elected to their position as representatives of each city, town and village assembly, so they are also responsible for creating pipelines that ensure that the needs of their localities are properly represented in the prefectural assembly. Another role they must play is to establish firm relationships with the leaders of their local constituencies.

② It goes without saying that the political stance of prefectural assembly members may differ from those of municipality leaders in such areas as political beliefs and party issues. There are many cases in which assembly members are required to work hard on modulating the political stance of their home constituencies, and this may have an adverse effect on the work they are expected to carry out as prefectural assembly members. There are currently calls for the actual role of prefectural assembly members to be reviewed.

③ Prefectural assembly members also represent the power base of their political party, and they are in a position in which they are able to have an enormous effect on party politics at the national level. Despite this, however, there is no doubt that their fundamental role as assembly members is to deliberate prefectural issues, and they are obliged to put their full weight behind this.

▶▶▶▶▶▶

[2] 都道府県議会議員の役割

❶ 都道府県の議会の役割は何でしょうか？ 議員は、基本的には市町村議会と同様に政策の審議、予算の承認、条例の制定などが主な仕事となります。また、議員は各市町村を単位とした選挙区で選出される場合が多いため、地域の要望などを都道府県全体に反映させるためのパイプ役という側面があります。各議員は、それぞれの地元の首長との連携も大切な役割なのです。

❷ もちろん政治信条の違いや政党の問題で、地元の首長と立場が違う場合もあります。その場合、地元との政治的な調整作業に尽力せざるをえない場合も多く、それが本来の議員としての仕事に悪影響を及ぼすこともあります。都道府県の議員はどうあるべきなのかを再度問い直すことが今求められています。

❸ また、都道府県議会議員は政党の基礎的な力になりますので、日本全体の政党政治に大きな影響を与える政治勢力ということもできます。しかし、いずれにせよ、議員の最も基本的な仕事は、都道府県政の審議であることは間違いなく、その充実が求められています。

[3] Becoming Prefectural Governor

① Standing as a candidate for prefectural governor is a huge career step for an assembly member. Governors have enormous power, with the budget for Tokyo, for example, being equal to the state finances for the whole of Canada. The responsibility that governors must shoulder is therefore great, and the qualifications for seeking election state that the candidate must be over 30 years of age and must pay a deposit of ¥3,000,000, which is the same as standing for a seat in the national Diet.

② The governor is nominally in charge of making sure that administrative operations are carried out smoothly, and in most cases they are political independents who run for the position with the recommendation of many different political parties, which seems, at a glance, to suggest that a single political party has minimal influence. In actual fact, however, the relationship between the ruling party and opposition parties is very complex, and there are cases in which their

influence has an effect on assembly operations.
　　　　　　　　～に影響を与える　　　　　議会運営

③ Also, the conditions for running for governor do not include
　　　　　　　　～の条件　　　　知事に立候補する　　　　　含まれない
the stipulation that the candidate must live within the area.
　　規定
This means that people well-known throughout the entire
　　　　　　　　　　　知名度の高い人　　　　　　全国を通じて
country sometimes stand for governor. For example, famous
　　　　　　　　　　～に立候補する　　　　　　　　　　　　　超有名人
celebrities became the governors of Miyazaki Prefecture and
Chiba Prefecture, and these elections attracted interest from
　　　　　　　　　　　　　　　　　　　　　　～から注目を集めた
throughout the whole country. Residents of the prefectures
　　　　　　　　　　　　　　　　　居住者
vote directly in the elections, in the same way as with city,
投票する　　　　　　　　　　　　　　～と同様に
town and village elections. This sometimes leads to cases
　　　　　　　　　　　　　　　　　　　　　　～につながる
in which governors who oppose the majority opinion of the
　　　　　　　　　　　　～と敵対する　大多数の意見
assembly being elected.
　　　　　選出された

▶▶▶▶▶▶

[3] 知事になる

❶ 議員から都道府県の知事に立候補することも政治家として大きなステップアップです。知事には大きな権限があり、予算規模でいえば、東京都はカナダの国家財政と同規模の予算を執行しています。よって、知事の責任は重く、被選挙権も30歳からとなっており、供託金も国会議員と同額の300万円となっています。

❷ 知事は行政運営をスムーズにする名目で、無所属で、多数の政党の推薦を受けて立候補する場合が多く、一見すると政党色は薄いのが現状です。しかし、県によっては、与野党の関係が複雑な場合もあり、それが議会運営に影響を与えることもあります。

❸ また、知事に立候補する条件としてその地域の住民である必要はありません。そのために全国的に知名度の高い人が知事に立候補する場合もあります。例えば宮崎県や千葉県の様に著名なタレントが知事になる場合もあり、その選挙は全国的に注目されます。選挙は市町村と同様で、県民の直接選挙です。その結果、議会の多数と対立する知事が生まれることもあります。

[4] Job of the Prefectural Governor

① The first job a governor must tackle is deciding on a vice-governor and other executives to decide administrative policy. Governors are extremely powerful, and in addition to having the right to dissolve the assembly, they also have the right to veto bylaws and budgets approved by the assembly, the right to establish unique taxes, such as tourism taxes (although these must be approved by the assembly and the Minister of Internal Affairs and Communications,) the right to manage personnel matters, the right to appoint members to some of the administrative committees, as well as the right to arbitrarily decide on a wide range of disciplinary measures.

② It is the job of the governor to use these rights as effectively as possible in order to contribute to the development of the region, and from the power that these rights invest in governors, it is obvious that it is a job that comes with extremely heavy responsibility. It is also a broad-reaching and very busy job, as it involves providing support for policies enacted by municipalities within the prefecture and coordinating with the central government on political policies.

③ Recently it is common for governors to become a symbol of the prefecture and to act as top salesmen in order to lure industry into the area, revitalize local industry, attract tourists and perform other such tasks, and they are required to prove their ability at spreading the word about the prefecture far and wide. The former governor of Miyazaki Prefecture, who was well known as being a TV celebrity, became famous for traveling around the country in order to sell prefectural produce. Given the level of responsibility that this job requires means that governors are prohibited from holding down other jobs at the same time, with the exception of acting as representatives for companies into which the prefecture has invested.

[4] 知事の仕事

❶ 知事になったら、まず、副知事などの執行部を決定し政策執行にあたります。知事の権限は非常に大きく、議会の解散権はもとより、議会で決定した条例や予算に対する拒否権、観光税など独自の租税の創設（議会の議決と総務大臣の認可が必要）、職員の人事権や一部の行政委員会の委員の任命権、様々な専決処分権限を有しています。

❷ こうした権限を有効に行使し、地域の発展に寄与することが知事の仕事であり、その権限の大きさから、責任も非常に大きな職であるといえます。また、都道府県内の各自治体の政策への支援や国との政策調整など、仕事の幅も広く多忙を極めます。

❸ 昨今では、企業誘致や地場産業の育成、観光誘致などに知事が都道府県の顔としてトップセールスを行うことも多く、その情報発信能力の手腕が問われます。一時タレント知事として有名になった宮崎県の知事が、県産品の売り出しに全国を飛び回ったことは有名です。なお、これだけ責任が重い職責のため、都道府県が出資した企業の代表などをのぞき、兼業は禁止されています。

[5] Main Issues Facing Today's Prefectural Administration

① Prefectures in Japan are currently facing a wide range of diversified issues. And, in the same way as cities, towns and villages, they are under pressure to return finances to a healthy state.

② Another large issue involves the eradication of disparities between regions. The economic disparities that exist between Tokyo, Osaka and other major metropolitan areas and rural regions continue to grow at a steady pace. This issue is getting so bad that the severity of various problems, such as the difficulty in maintaining medical standards, is being pointed out for rural areas. Improving regional economies through the governor acting as a salesman and establishing infrastructures for transportation, etc., are important elements in eradicating these problems.

③ However, there is a history of prefectures being pressured to use finances to create unnecessary infrastructures in the past, so it is very important to maintain a good balance between revenue, demand and the value of investment, etc. Also, rural areas face a wide range of issues unique to the area, such as the problem of "*genkai shuraku*," or communities in which the majority of residents are senior citizens, and the problem of slimming down administrative organizations that have become bloated, so it is necessary for the prefectural assembly to establish close communications with the cities, towns and villages in question in order to solve these problems.

▶▶▶▶▶

[5] 都道府県政の課題

❶ 現在、都道府県が抱える課題は多岐にわたります。市町村などと同様、財政の健全化が差し迫った課題です。

❷ また、地域格差の解消も大きな問題です。現在、東京や大阪といった大都市と、地方の経済的格差はどんどん大きくなっています。地方では、医療のレベルを維持することなどにも深刻な問題が指摘されるほどです。そうした問題の解消のためにも、知事のトップセールスや、交通等のインフラ整備などにより地域経済を向上させることが大切なのです。

❸ しかし、過去に必要とは思えないインフラを作り財政を圧迫した経緯もあり、財源と需要や投資価値などのバランスをとっていくことが重要です。また、高齢化による限界集落の問題、肥大化した行政機構のスリム化、教育問題など、地域独特の問題が多岐にわたり、該当する市町村と提携しながら問題解決にあたる必要があります。

④ There are also prefectures facing problems that involve the central government, such as the US military base issue in Okinawa Prefecture, and the methods of establishing communications with the government and reflecting regional assertions onto nationwide policy are being called into question.

[5] 都道府県政の課題　つづき
❹ 地域によっては沖縄県の基地問題など、国政にも大きく関わる問題もあり、そこでは国との関係をどう構築し、地域の主張を全国的に反映していくかが問われています。

Chapter 2
National Diet Members

▶▶▶▶▶▶▶

第2章　国会議員

1▶ Becoming a Member of the National Diet
国会議員になる

[1] What are Diet Members?

① And finally, running for a seat in the national Diet is an important step for becoming Prime Minister. In order to do this, it is necessary to have a full understanding of the way in which the Diet is configured.

② The seat of national government in Japan is split into two assemblies. This is known as the two-house system. The first of these houses is known as the House of Representatives, and the second one is known as the House of Councillors. The House of Representatives was established under the Meiji Constitution before World War II. The House of Councillors was established after World War II in accordance with the Constitution of Japan when the pre-war House of Peers was abolished.

③ The period of tenure in the House of Representatives is four years, but the Prime Minister retains the power to disband the house at any time. The period of tenure in the House of Councillors is six years, and it cannot be disbanded midway through these periods. However, elections are held every three years, with half of the entire house membership requiring to be reelected.

④ Incidentally, the House of Representatives elections are known as general elections, and the House of Councillors elections are known as triennial elections. Eligibility for election requires candidates for the House of Representatives to be 25 years of age or older, and candidates for the House of Councillors to be 30 years of age or older. The period of tenure for the House of Representatives is short and the assembly can be disbanded at any time, so it is thought to be more effective at reflecting the opinions of the general public directly, and it is therefore considered superior in status to the House of Councillors with respect to receiving the nomination for becoming Prime Minister and for settling budgets, etc.

⑤ The period of tenure for the House of Councillors is longer, which provides more time for carefully considering the policy bills placed before it, and it is therefore also known as the "House of Reason" and the "House of Common Sense."

提供する　　　　　　　　　　　　　　　　　法案
提起される
理性の府
良識の府

The Diet Building
国会議事堂

The Diet Building was completed in 1936. It has a symmetrical design. The House of Councillors is on the right side.
議事堂は1936年に完成し、左右対称。向かって右が参議院

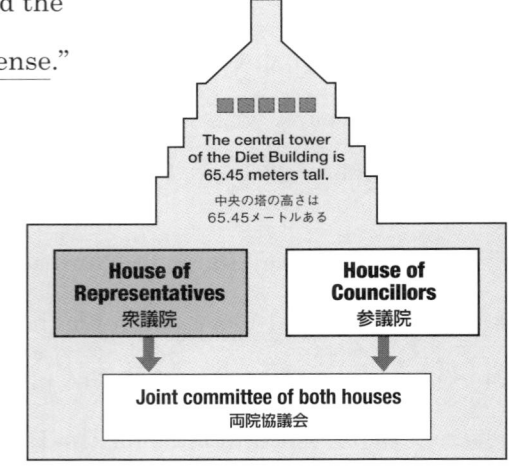

The central tower of the Diet Building is 65.45 meters tall.
中央の塔の高さは65.45メートルある

House of Representatives 衆議院
House of Councillors 参議院
Joint committee of both houses 両院協議会

▶▶▶▶▶

[1] 国会議員とは

❶ いよいよ、内閣総理大臣になるための重要なステップ、国会議員に立候補します。そのためには国会の仕組みを十分理解することが必要です。

❷ 日本には国政に関する議会が2つあります。これを二院制議会といいます。一つは衆議院、もう一つは参議院です。衆議院は戦前の大日本帝国憲法下で成立した議院です。参議院は戦後、日本国憲法により戦前の貴族院を廃止して創設された議院です。

❸ 衆議院の任期は4年ですが、内閣総理大臣によっていつでも解散することができます。参議院の任期は6年で、任期途中の解散はありません。ただ、選挙は3年おきで、全体の半数ずつ改選していきます。

❹ ちなみに衆議院議員選挙のことを総選挙、参議院議員選挙のことを通常選挙と呼びます。また被選挙権は衆議院が25歳以上、参議院は30歳以上です。衆議院は任期が短く解散もあるので直接民意を反映しやすいとされ、内閣総理大臣の指名、予算決定などで衆議院が参議院より優越しています。

❺ 参議院は任期が長いため、政策をじっくりと考えていくことが可能なため、「理性の府」「良識の府」と呼ばれています。

[2] Standing for the National Diet

① Standing for a seat in the National Diet requires potential candidates to decide whether they want to enter the House of Representatives or the House of Councillors. As mentioned in the previous section, the period of tenure and the levels of authority granted differ between the House of Representatives and the House of Councillors. It is also thought more effective to join the House of Representatives if the candidate wishes to receive a nomination to become Prime Minister.

② Although it is possible for members of the House of Councillors to become Prime Minister from a legal viewpoint, there are no cases of members of the House of Councillors being elected to Prime Minister in post-war Japan. The reasons for this are said to include the fact that the Prime Minister only has the authority to disband the House of Representatives, and that the term of tenure for the House of Representatives is short and it is therefore more effective at reflecting the most recent opinions of the general public.

③ Having decided on the house to run for, it is then necessary to decide which constituency to represent. It is possible to run for any constituency, regardless of whether the candidate is resident there or not. The remaining procedure for standing as a candidate involves paying a deposit of ¥3,000,000.

④ In the same way as with municipal elections, it is necessary for candidates to be Japanese nationals and be in possession of all civil rights. Although it is possible to run for a seat in the National Diet as an independent, most candidates run under the official recognition of political parties. It is also necessary for both House of Representatives and House of Councillors candidates to be backed by a political party when standing for a proportional representation constituency. It is therefore necessary to select a political party that echoes the candidate's own political stance. Also, having received the official backing of a political party, the candidate will be expected to champion the manifest of that party. If this is thought to be difficult, then the candidate must run as an independent.

I wish you would show better sense.

If worst comes to worst, we may force our decisions through regardless of you.

良識をもって行動してくださいよ

いざとなったら強行採決さけないぞ!!

House of Representatives　　　　House of Councillors

> One of the House of Councillors' functions is to encourage members of the House of Representatives to take a balanced approach.
> 参議院は衆議院の行き過ぎを抑える

▶▶▶▶▶

[2] 国会議員に出馬

❶ 国会議員に立候補する場合、衆議院にするか参議院にするかを決めなくてはなりません。前項の通り、衆議院と参議院では任期や権限が異なります。また、内閣総理大臣を目指すならば衆議院の方が良いと思われます。

❷ 法律上では参議院議員でも、内閣総理大臣になることは可能ですが、戦後参議院議員が総理になった例はありません。これは、内閣総理大臣の解散権が衆議院に対してのみであることと、衆議院は任期が短く、直近の民意を反映しやすいと言われていることなどによります。

❸ 議院を決めたら選挙区を決めます。選挙区は、自分が住んでいる場所に関わりなく決定することができます。そして300万円の供託金を納めて立候補する段取りになります。

❹ 立候補には自治体の選挙と同様に日本国籍と公民権が必要です。国会議員の場合、無所属でもかまいませんが、多くの場合、政党の公認で出馬します。さらに比例区への立候補は衆参とも政党である必要があります。よって、自分の主張にあう政党を選定する必要があるでしょう。また、政党の公認を受けた以上、その政党のマニフェストを主張することになります。それが難しければ無所属での立候補となります。

2 ▶ Political Parties
政党

[1] History of Japan's Political Parties

① The number of political parties maintaining a presence in the National Diet stands at thirteen as of April 2013, including the Liberal Democratic Party, the Democratic Party of Japan, the Japan Restoration Party and the New Komeito Party. Factions affiliated to political parties are formed in the houses.

② In post-war Japan, political parties were established in accordance with political ideologies. The Liberal Democratic Party is a right-wing conservative party that followed in the path of the conservative party stance that was popular before the war, the Social Democratic Party of Japan descended from the Japan Socialist Party, and the Japanese Communist Party was originally a left-wing reformist party.

③ The Liberal Democratic Party and the Japan Socialist Party are the two major parties that led the National Diet after the war. Following this, centrist parties, such as the New Komeito Party, which is affiliated to a religious organization, and the Democratic Socialist Party, which broke away from the Japan Socialist Party, were established as a counterbalance to ideology-based parties, and the formation of the Democratic Party of Japan, which consists of a collection of groups that splintered away from the Liberal Democratic Party and the Japan Socialist Party, have led

Subsidies for political parties
政党交付金

Under the Party Subsidies Law, the national government provides financial support for political parties that satisfy certain conditions, such as the number of affiliated Diet members and the percentage of votes they receive in national elections. The parties also have to be registered corporations.

「政党助成法」に基づき、政党の活動費を国が補助することになった。
所属国会議員数や国政選挙の得票率などで一定の用件を満たし、
法人登記をした政党がこの交付金を受け取れる

Distributed three times per year
年3回に分けて交付

Work hard for the people!

国民のためにしっかりお願いね

250 yen per citizen
国民1人当たり
負担金250円

National Treasury
国庫

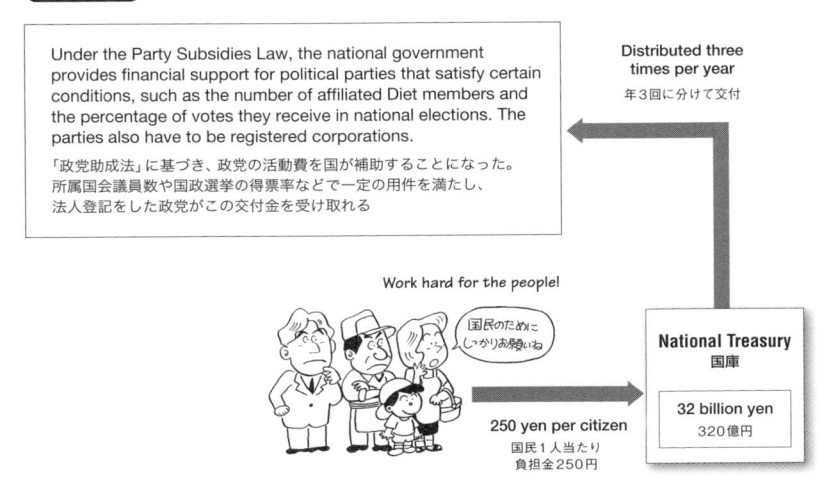

32 billion yen
320億円

to a watering-down of the sense of ideology that used to be prevalent in political parties.

④ The two current major political parties are the Liberal Democratic Party and the Democratic Party of Japan. The Liberal Democratic Party is clearly a conservative party, and the Democratic Party of Japan is seen as having a wide coverage that leans slightly toward reformism.

Companies, labor unions, and other large contributors can donate money only to political parties and their fund-raising groups. They cannot contribute to individual politicians.
企業や労働組合などが大口献金をする場合は、政党・政党の政治資金団体だけに限られ、個人献金はできない

The names of recipients must be made public.
献金先を公開しなければなりません

Company   Party
Over 50,000 yen per party

▶▶▶▶▶▶

[1] 日本の政党の歴史
❶ 現在、国会議員を出している政党は、自由民主党、民主党、日本維新の会、公明党など、2013年4月現在で13党あります。議院ではこの政党を母体に会派を結成します。

❷ 戦後の日本では、政治イデオロギーで政党が結成されてきました。戦前からの保守政党の流れを汲む自民党は保守右派政党、社民党の前身である社会党、共産党は革新左派政党でした。

❸ 特に自民党と社会党は戦後の2大政党として国会を牽引してきました。こうしたイデオロギー政党に対して、その後、宗教団体を母体とした公明党や社会党から離脱した民社党などが中道政党として成立し、現在では自民党や社会党から分離したグループを糾合した民主党などが結成されたことで、政党のイデオロギー色は薄まりました。

❹ 現在の2大政党は自民党と民主党です。自民党は明らかに保守政党ですが、民主党は幅が広くやや革新よりということができる程度です。

[2] The Liberal Democratic Party

① The Liberal Democratic Party, which is currently in power, basically has high levels of affinity with the fields of business and finance, and concentrates its policies on economic growth that reflects the intentions of business circles. It therefore establishes policies that are mainly aimed at liberalization through deregulation and public investment, etc.

② With regards to overseas diplomacy, its main policy is to cooperate with the United States of America, and it is adheres firmly to the Treaty of Mutual Cooperation and Security between the United States and Japan. Its fundamental stance on defense is to maintain substantiated Self-Defense Forces. It is a conservative party ideology-wise that actively supports the merits of the Emperor system and the Japanese family system, etc.

③ The Liberal Democratic Party's conservative stance means that it espouses thorough levels of moral education, etc. Revising the Constitution has long been a dream of the Liberal Democratic Party, and the revisions it calls mainly are items related to the sovereignty of the Emperor, the placement of national defense forces and the right to collective defense, and the relationship between rights and obligations.

④ Although Liberal Democratic Party policies are achieving success from an economic standpoint, they are criticized for creating a situation in which it is easy for cozy relationships between politics and business to be established. With regard to the party's awareness of history, there are also many cases in which it tends to have a very affirmative view of Japan's position during World War II, which causes friction with other Asian nations. It enjoys strong ties with regional politics and regional industry and provides support for economic growth in rural areas, which generates criticism over public investment that is not deemed to be necessary.

[2] 自由民主党

❶ 現在の政権与党自民党は、基本的に財界と親和性が高く、財界の意向に添った経済成長路線を政策の中心に置いています。そのために、規制緩和による様々な自由化、公共投資などを中心に政策を立てています。

❷ 外交では、対アメリカ協調路線を主軸とし、日米安保条約を堅持しています。防衛政策としては自衛隊の充実が基本政策です。思想、イデオロギー的には保守的で、天皇制や日本の家族制度などに積極的な価値を考えています。

❸ 教育政策などでも、その保守的な性格から道徳教育の充実などを主張しています。憲法改正は長年の自民党の悲願で、天皇の元首化、国防軍の設置と集団的自衛権の容認、権利義務関係の見直しなどを主な主張としています。

❹ こうした自民党の政策は経済的には成功を収めますが、財界との癒着を生みやすく批判されます。また、歴史認識において、第二次世界大戦における日本の立場を肯定的に見る場合が多く、アジア諸国と軋轢を生むケースがあります。地方政治や地方財界とのつながりが強く、地方の経済発展を支える傍ら、必要と思えない公共投資をする場合もあり、この点も批判されています。

[3] The Democratic Party of Japan

① The Democratic Party of Japan was critical of public investment, cozy relationships between the government and business, bureaucratic rule and other issues when the Liberal Democratic Party was in power, and it rode a wave of public expectation during the 2009 general election to claim victory and bring about a change in government. However, a large number of clumsy gaffs in running the administration cooled off the expectations of the public, and they lost the 2012 general election and were forced back out into the opposition.

② The basic policies of the Democratic Party of Japan champion the general populace and focus on lifestyle rehabilitation through improved welfare and household finances, etc. It maintains high levels of affinity with labor unions and similar organizations, and Rengo (Japan Trade Union Confederation) and other labor organizations tend to support it in principle.

③ Its other basic policies include abolishing bureaucratic

rule through political reform, cutting down on the amount of public investment funds being wasted, economic growth through reforms in the economic system, and the promotion of environmental conservation.

④ With regard to overseas diplomacy, although it admits that Japan-US relations are extremely important, its policies basically place the emphasis on Asia, and its fundamental stance with regard to defense policies is to maintain the status quo. The party's current stance on the Constitution leans toward maintaining it in its current state.

▶▶▶▶▶▶

[3] 民主党

❶ 民主党は自民党政権時代の公共投資の問題や財界との癒着、官僚支配などを批判し、2009年の総選挙で国民の期待に乗って大勝し、政権交代を実現しました。しかし、政権運営に不手際が多く、国民の期待もさめ、2012年の総選挙で惨敗し野に下りました。

❷ 民主党の基本的な主張は国民目線での生活再建で、福祉の充実や家計の向上などが基本的な政策になります。これは労働組合などと親和性が高く、連合などの労働団体は民主党の基本的な支援団体です。

❸ また、行政改革による官僚支配の打破や、無駄な公共投資の抑制、経済制度改革による経済成長、さらには環境保護の推進などが基本的な政策になります。

❹ 外交では日米関係の重要性は認めながらも、アジアを重視した政策を基本に持っており、防衛政策も基本的には現状維持を基本としています。憲法に関しても、現状ではやや護憲よりです。

[4] Other Political Parties

① The New Komeito Party, which has formed a coalition with the Liberal Democratic Party, is affiliated to a religious organization. The New Komeito Party's basic policies include promoting welfare, protecting small- to medium-sized companies, and realizing peace, and they are cautious about revising the Constitution. A future point of interest will be whether it will be possible for the party to maintain the coalition in light of the Liberal Democratic Party's stance on the issue of the Constitution.

② The parties that are considered to wield the most power within the field of politics in the future are the conservative Japan Restoration Party and the Your Party. These parties are separated on the issues of massive structural reform to the economy and on bureaucratic government, but they mostly advocate revising the Constitution, etc. However, there is a possibility that these parties are simply enjoying popularity as a temporary fad, so it is necessary to

keep a close eye on their future movements.
~を見守る   今後の動向

③ The parties that are against revising the Constitution include the People's Life Party, the Social Democratic Party and the Japanese Communist Party. In particular, the ideology of the Social Democratic Party and the Japanese Communist Party is especially left-wing reformist, but both parties are currently experiencing a continuing period of decline.

[4] その他の政党

❶ 自民党と連立を組んでいるのが宗教団体を母体とする公明党です。公明党は福祉の増進、中小企業の保護、平和の実現などが基本的な主張で、憲法改正には慎重です。今後、憲法問題などで自民党との連立を維持できるかがポイントになります。

❷ 今後の政界で大きく影響力を握ると思われているのが、保守系の日本維新の会とみんなの党です。これらの党は政治経済の大胆な構造改革、官僚政治との決別、憲法改正などを主な主張としています。ただ、ブームの様な側面もあり、今後の動向に注意が必要です。

❸ 憲法に関する護憲勢力は生活の党、社会民主党、日本共産党などです。特に社会民主党と日本共産党はイデオロギー的には左派革新政党ということができますが、両党とも現在は長期退潮が続いています。

3 Elections
選挙

[1] House of Representatives Election

① The election for seats in the House of Representatives is known as a general election. Candidates must be 25 years of age or older. The decisions made in the House of Representatives take precedence with regard to the vote on nominating Prime Ministers in the Diet, and the Prime Minister is usually nominated from the party with the majority in the House of Representatives.

② Because of this, general elections are also elections for selecting the government. The term of tenure in the House of Representatives in four years, but the Prime Minister retains the right to disband the house, so elections to reelect a government can technically be held at any time.

③ There are a total of 480 seats in the house, and an electoral system comprised of single-seat constituencies and proportionally represented multiple-seat constituencies is currently in effect. This entails one candidate being elected from 300 single-seat constituencies, and 180 candidates being elected from a total of eleven multiple-seat constituencies spread throughout the country. Running for election in both single-seat constituencies and proportionally represented multiple-seat constituencies is acceptable, so in addition to the proportional representation candidacy list announced by the parties, the system also allows for candidates who lost the vote by a small proportional margin in single-seat constituencies to get another chance to be elected in proportional representation constituencies. The candidates who achieve this are then registered in the proportional representation candidacy list.

④ This system came into being for the purpose of minimizing wasted votes, which are said to be the flaw in single-seat constituencies. The disparity between each vote in metropolitan areas and agricultural areas is currently great, and some constituencies are claiming that this system is in violation of the Constitution, which demands equality under the law. Attention is now focused on what will happen to the election system in the future in light of this situation.

How Diet members are elected — House of Representatives
議員選出のしくみ ──衆議院

Single-seat constituencies 小選挙区選出	Proportional representation 比例代表選出
Between 2 and 25 Diet members are chosen by each prefecture. 都道府県ごとに2〜25の選挙区に分けて議員を選出	The country is divided into 11 blocks, each of which chooses between 7 and 33 Diet members. 全国を11のブロックに分け、7〜33名の議員を選出
300 members 300名	**180 members** 180名

They are elected to four-year terms, but they lose their seats when the Diet is dissolved.
任期は4年だが、解散によって資格を失う

[1] 衆議院議員選挙

❶ 衆議院議員選挙は、「総選挙」と呼ばれています。被選挙権は25歳以上です。国会で行われる首相指名のおりに衆議院の議決が優先されるため、通常は衆議院の第一党から内閣総理大臣が指名されます。

❷ そのため、総選挙は政権選択選挙の面もあります。衆議院の任期は4年ですが、内閣総理大臣には衆議院の解散権があるため、常に選挙の可能性があります。

❸ 定数は480で、現在の選挙制度は小選挙区比例代表並立制が採用されています。これは300選挙区から1名ずつ選出する小選挙区と、全国11の比例代表区で180名を選出します。小選挙区と比例代表には重複立候補が認められており政党の定める比例順位の他、小選挙区で落選した候補者の惜敗率で復活当選ができる制度になっています。その対象者は同一の比例順位で届け出がされています。

❹ この制度は、小選挙区の欠点と言われる死票をできるだけ少なくするために生まれた制度です。現在、都市部と農村部の一票の格差が大きく、一部の選挙区では法の下の平等を定めた憲法に抵触するとして違憲判決が出ています。こうした事情で、今後この選挙制度がどうなるか、注目されています。

[2] House of Councillors Election

① The election for seats in the House of Councillors is known as a regular election. Candidates must be 30 years of age or older. The term of tenure for the House of Councillors is six years, and half of the house members are reelected once every three years. The House of Councillors cannot be disbanded, so the election dates do not fluctuate.

② Because the House of Councillors cannot be disbanded and the term of tenure is long, it is said that it is capable of debating policy with a long-term view and without being influenced by temporary moods. Candidates also tend to champion their policies based on this long-term view during their election activities.

③ The house contains 242 seats, and 121 members, or half of the total, need to be reelected during elections. The electoral system provides 73 seats from prefectural constituencies, and another 48 proportional representation seats from throughout the country. The number of seats available for prefectural constituencies differs depending on population demographics, with between one seat and five seats up for grabs per prefecture.

④ Many prefectures only have one seat, which in reality means that they are single-seat constituencies. The prefecture with the largest number of seats is Tokyo, with five seats. It is possible to vote for candidates under their individual names or their political party names in proportional representation constituencies, and the total number of votes received for both individual names and party names grants the party a seat in the house. The order of proportional representation candidacy uses the open list method in which candidate with the most individual votes being elected, and candidates who are well-known throughout the country are thought to have an advantage.

How Diet members are elected — House of Councillors
議員選出のしくみ —— 参議院

Prefectural voting
選挙区選出

Members of the upper house are chosen from 47 districts, one for each prefecture.

全国を都道府県ごとに47選挙区に分けて議員を選出（地方区）

142 members
142名

Proportional representation
比例代表選出

Voters cast ballots for individual candidates and political parties in a combined format, with those elected being decided in the order of greatest number of votes.

個人名と政党名を併用した投票方式で、得票数の多い順に当選者が決まる

100 members
100名

Councillors serve six-year terms. Every three years, elections are held for half of the seats.
任期は6年で、3年ごとに半数を改選

[2] 参議院議員選挙

❶ 参議院議員選挙は、「通常選挙」と呼ばれています。被選挙権は30歳以上です。参議院議員の任期は6年で、3年に一度、議員の半数ずつが改選されます。参議院には解散がありませんので、選挙日程は変わりません。

❷ 参議院は解散がなく、任期も長いため、一時のムードではなく、長期的視野に立って政策を議論することができると言われています。選挙でも、候補者はそうした視点で政策を訴えていく傾向があります。

❸ 定数は242人で、半数改選である選挙の際は121人が改選されることになります。選挙制度は各都道府県別の選挙区から73議席を選出し、それとは別に全国一律の比例代表により48議席が選出されます。都道府県別の選挙区はその地域の人口との兼ね合いで、定数が1から5まで違いがあります。

❹ 多くの県は定数が1で事実上の小選挙区です。最大の選挙区は東京で定数は5となります。比例区は個人名でも政党名でも投票ができ、個人票と政党票の合算で政党に議席が割り振られます。比例順位は個人票の票数に応じて当選していく非拘束名簿方式で全国的に知名度の高い候補者が有利とされています。

4　The House
議院

[1] The Job of Diet Members

① Candidates who are elected in National Diet elections are in charge of being directly involved in national policy. Scenes of newly-elected candidates entering the Diet for the first time are regularly covered by the media, and many of the new Diet members have commemorative photographs taken.

② However, they shoulder the expectations of everyone in the country so cannot rest on their laurels at being newly elected, and they must approach their work with responsibility in the same way as experienced members.

③ The first job they have as Diet members is to vote in the election nominating the Prime Minister. This basically calls for them to vote for the leader of the party to which they are affiliated, but if that the party leader fails to gain the majority of votes, a play-off vote between the top two nominees is carried out.

④ In addition to the Prime Minister nomination, the work of Diet members includes taking part in heated debates in the Diet, and debating issues in the various committees that they join (Budget Committee, Committee on Judicial Affairs, etc.) The issues on which they need to pass resolutions are diverse and many, and their job encompasses everything from deliberating the national budget, legislature and treaties through to making proposals with regard to revising the Constitution, etc.

⑤ Diet Members have the right to initiate parliamentary investigations, and are able to investigate anything at all pertaining to national policy. Also, in order to prevent members being suppressed by the government as a result of their political activities, the right to be absolved of all responsibility outside of the house for the statements they make before the Diet, and the right

to parliamentary immunity from arrest while the Diet is
議員不逮捕特権
in session are protected by the Constitution.
開会中　　　〜によって保護されている

Member's Compensation
議員の特権

Salary in the top civil-servant pay bracket
公務員としての最高額レベルの給与
歳費を受ける権利

免責特権
Immunity for statements and votes

Whatever I say in the Diet is OK!
国会内での発言

文書通信交通滞在費
月額100万円
1,000,000 yen monthly for communication, transportation, work-related accommodation.

不逮捕特権
Immunity from arrest

立法事務委託費
月額65万円
Expenditures for Legislative Activities: 650,000 yen a Month

アシ代優待
Transportation privileges

現行犯以外は、会期中は逮捕されない
Diet members cannot be arrested during a Diet session unless caught in the act.

▶▶▶▶▶▶

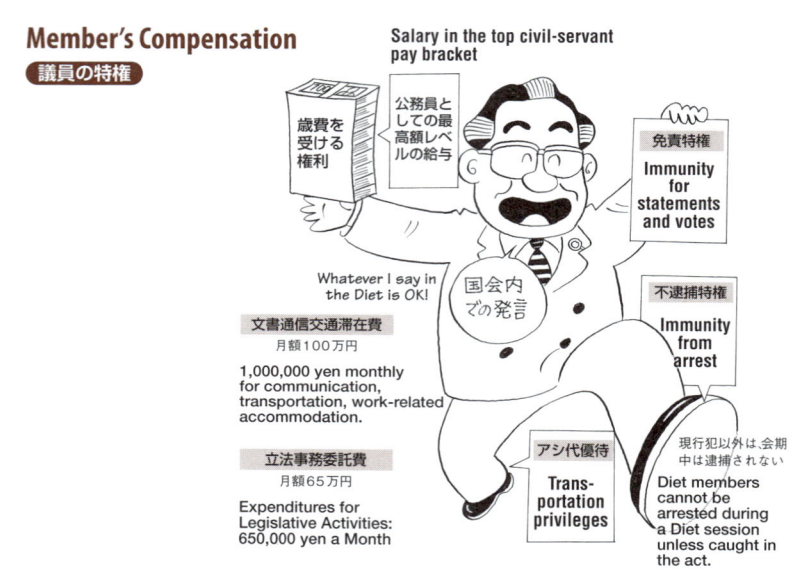

[1] 国会議員の仕事

❶ 国会議員選挙に出馬し当選したら、国政に直接関与する仕事に就くことになります。選挙後の初登院の様子はよくマスコミで報道され、記念写真を撮る新人議員も多くいます。

❷ しかし、新人といえども国民の負託をうけた国会議員なので、ベテランと同様大きな責任の中で仕事をすることになります。

❸ 国会議員として最初の仕事は首相指名選挙の投票です。基本的には自分の属する政党の党首に投票することになりますが、過半数の得票がない場合は、上位2名での決選投票となります。

❹ 首相指名以降の仕事は、国会論戦になりますが、各議員は様々な委員会（予算委員会、法務委員会など）に属し、そこで議論するのが仕事です。議決内容は、予算、法律、条約の審議から憲法改正の発議など多岐にわたります。

❺ 国会議員は国政調査権という大きな権限を持ち、国政に関する事柄を何でも調べることができます。また、こうした政治活動で政府の弾圧を受けないため、国会での発言は、院外で責任を問われないことや、国会開会中の不逮捕特権などが憲法で認められています。

[2] Resolving Matters in the Diet

① The Diet is largely divided into four sessions. The most important of these is the ordinary session, which is convened for a period of 150 days from January and holds debates centering mostly on the national budget.

② In addition to this there are extraordinary sessions, which are convened when the government deems it necessary and when more than one quarter of Diet members issue a request, special sessions, which are convened within thirty days of a general election to nominate the Prime Minister, and emergency sessions, which are convened by the House of Councillors in order to deal with emergencies when the House of Representatives has been disbanded.

③ Legislative bills placed before the Diet that are not subject to the procedures for continual debate while the Diet is in session and for which no resolution is made by the end of debate are discarded, and in principle the same bill may not be resubmitted during a different session.

④ Legislative bills pass the Diet only after they have been approved by the majority of committee members, after they have been approved by the majority of Diet members during the ordinary session, and after they have been approved by similar procedures after being sent to the other house (the House of Councillors if submitted originally to the House of Representatives).

⑤ In the event of both houses reaching different decisions, ten representatives are selected from both houses to form a bi-house council. The decision of the House of Representatives takes precedence over bills related to the nomination of Prime Minister and the budget and these bills are enacted if no decision is reached even after this, and regular bills are enacted only if two-thirds of the House of Representatives vote in favor.

⑥ Bills calling for the revision of the Constitution will be enacted if two-thirds of both houses vote in favor, and if one-half of the electorate vote in favor during a national referendum.

Bills that are rejected as a result of these procedures are
         否決された
discarded, and they may not be resubmitted again for
deliberation.
審議

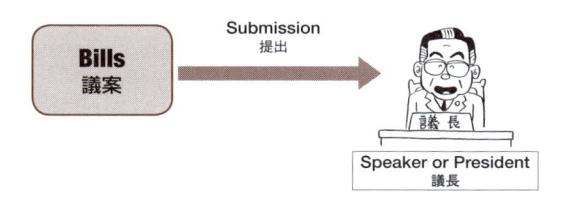

A bill is submitted by a Diet member or committee, and may be submitted to either House first, but budget proposals must go through the House of Representatives first.
議案提出は、国会議員、委員会が行い、衆・参どちらの議院でもよいが、予算案は衆議院が優先

▶▶▶▶▶

[2] 国会の決議方法

❶ 国会には大きく分けて４つの会議があります。最も重要なのが通常国会で、１月から150日間の会期で行われ、特に予算を中心に論戦が行われます。

❷ 他は、内閣が必要と認めた、もしくは国会議員４分の１以上の要求があった場合に行われる臨時国会、総選挙後30日以内に内閣総理大臣指名のために行われる特別国会、そして、衆議院の解散中の緊急事態に対応するために行われる参議院の緊急集会です。

❸ 国会で上程された法案は、会期中に継続審議の手続きをせずに審議未了などで議決されない場合は廃案になり、同じ案を別の国会で再上程することは原則できません。

❹ 法案は、まず委員会の過半数で議決した後に、国会本会議の過半数で議決し、別の院（衆議院議決ならば参議院）に送られ、同様の手続きで議決されれば成立となります。

❺ ２つの院で異なる議決がされた場合は、各院から10名ずつの代表を出して両院評議会を開きます。そこでも決まらない場合は、首相指名、予算関連の案件は、衆議院の議決が優先されそのまま成立し、一般法案は衆議院の３分の２の賛成で再議決した場合のみ成立します。

❻ 憲法改正は両院の３分の２の議決の他、国民投票で２分の１の賛成で成立します。こうした手続きの結果、否決された案件は廃案となり、再上程はできません。

[3] The House of Representatives

① The House of Representatives takes precedence over the House of Councillors and is the most important house in the Diet (highest organ of state power). The Speaker of the House of Representatives is on an equal footing with the Prime Minister and Chief Justice of the Supreme Court, who are invested with the so-called "three powers" of government (administrative power, legislative power, and judicial power). The Speaker of the House is usually selected from the ruling party, and the vice-Speaker of the House is usually selected from the most powerful opposition party. It is customary for the Speaker of the House to leave his/her party upon commencing his/her duties.

② Members of the House of Representatives are commonly assigned to the positions of Ministers of State, vice-Ministers of State and parliamentary officials owing to the fact that they are in a position to determine state policy, and, with the exception of the Prime Minister, 15 of the 18 Ministers of State and 20 of the 25 vice-Minsters of State in the current cabinet (Abe cabinet) are members of the House of Representatives.

③ Seventeen standing committees permanently exist within the House of Representatives. The Budget Committee, with 50 members, is the largest, and the Disciplinary Committee, with 20 members, is the smallest. The total number of members in these 17 committees provides them with the power of majority within the house, and as the posts of the committee chairmen thereby control the 252 available seats to provide what is known as a "stable majority," it is these posts that the ruling party aims at in elections.

④ Also, if the government can secure a two-thirds—or 320-seat—majority in the house, which will enable it to pass bills that were rejected by the House of Councillors and revise the Constitution, all of the policies submitted to the house for debate by the government can be passed, which will facilitate the smooth running of government. However, enabling

the party in power to do anything it wishes is thought to be a
　　政権与党　　　　　　　　　何でもする　　　望む
problem that flies in the face of the concept of democracy.
　　　　　　～と相反する　　　　　　　　民主主義の概念

House of Representatives
衆議院の優越事項

If the two Houses reach different decisions, a joint committee is formed to work out a compromise. If a middle ground cannot be found, the decision of the House of Representatives takes precedence in the case of: • Proposed legislation • Budgets • Approval of treaties • Appointment of the Prime Minister • No-confidence votes, and the dissolution of the House of Representatives	衆議院と参議院が異なった議決をした場合は、両院協議会で話し合いが行われるが、それでもまとまらないときは、衆議院の議決が参議院の議決に優先して国会の議決となる • 法律案 • 予算案 • 条約の承認 • 内閣総理大臣の指名 • 内閣不信任→解散（衆議院のみ）

▶▶▶▶▶

[3] 衆議院

❶ 衆議院は参議院に優越するため、国会（国権の最高機関）において最も重要な院です。衆議院議長は内閣総理大臣、最高裁判所長官と並び、三権（立法権／行政権／司法権）の長とされます。通常、衆議院議長は第一党から、副議長は野党第一党から選出され、議長職に就くと、慣例として出身政党から離党します。

❷ 衆議院議員は、政権を選択する院でもあるため、国務大臣、副大臣、政務官などに就任する場合が多く、現在の内閣（安倍内閣）でも内閣総理大臣をのぞく18名の大臣のうち15名、25名の副大臣のうち20名が衆議院議員です。

❸ 衆議院には17の常設委員会があり、委員数50名の予算委員会が最大で、最小は20名の懲罰委員会です。この17の委員会の全てで半数以上の勢力を維持し、委員長のポストが取れる252議席を安定多数と呼び、与党は選挙の目標としてきました。

❹ また、参議院で否決した法案の再可決や憲法改正が可能となる3分の2、320議席を確保すると、与党の出した政策は理論上全て成立することになり、政権運営は容易になります。しかし、その場合、与党は何でもできることになり、民主主義としては問題があると考えられています。

[4] The House of Councillors

① The House of Councillors creates a rather humble impression owing to the fact that the House of Representatives takes precedence over it in a variety of ways. However, members of the House of Councillors have the same rights as members of the House of Representatives in their capacity as Diet members. It is not possible to dissolve the House of Councillors and the members are guaranteed a six-year tenure, and when this is coupled with the fact that the house contains members who are elected on a proportional representation ticket covering the entire country instead of just being tied to a single constituency, it is said that this house is able to carefully consider the most ideal policies without being affected by temporary fads. It is also thought to be advantageous in making it difficult for regional pork-barrel policies to be passed.

② It is because of these characteristics that the House of Councillors is also known as the "House of Reason" and the "House of Common Sense." Despite this, the House of Councillors is also sometimes labeled a carbon copy of the House of Representatives when political parties gain similar levels of power, and labeled as a hindrance to running the government when the balance of power shifts the other way (when the number of house members affiliated to the ruling party are in the minority), and there are even calls for the House of Councillors to be abolished.

③ However, the two-house system consisting of the House of Representatives and the House of Councillors that Japan has adopted is recognized as being a significant system for ensuring that the national government is run carefully without being affected by temporary fads and political momentum, and it is thought that the House of Councillors will never be abolished.

[4] 参議院

❶ 参議院は様々な面で衆議院が優越するために、地味な印象があります。しかし、参議院議員も、衆議院議員と同じ国会議員として平等な権限があります。参議院は解散がなく、6年の任期が保証されている点、地域のしがらみに関係のない全国一斉の比例区で選出された議員がいる点などで、一時期のブームに左右されることなく、じっくりと理想的な政策を考えていくことができると言われています。地域の利益誘導などが生じにくいのも利点とされます。

❷ こうした特徴をもって、参議院を「理性の府」、「良識の府」と呼ぶ場合もあります。ただ、衆議院と各政党の勢力が似てくると、衆議院のカーボンコピーと言われ、勢力が逆の場合（参議院では少数与党の場合）は政策運営の障害とされるなど、参議院の廃止論が出てくることが多いのも事実です。

❸ しかし、日本が衆議院と参議院という二院制をとっていることは、ブームや勢いが国政を左右することなく、慎重に国政を行うことに意義を認めているので、今後も参議院が無くなることはないと考えられます。

Chapter 3
The Government

▶▶▶▶▶▶▶
第3章 政府

1 ▶ The Prime Minister
内閣総理大臣

[1] Becoming the Prime Minister

① The leader of the cabinet in power in Japan is generally referred to as the Prime Minister. The Prime Minister holds ultimate responsibility for Japan's government, and is therefore the most powerful person in the country. It is a job that establishes the Prime Minister as the head of state.

② The Constitution of Japan states that the Diet is the highest organ of state power, which can be interpreted as the Speaker of the House of Representatives being the head of Japan from a constitutional viewpoint, but in actual fact it is more practical to consider the Prime Minister as being the head of state.

③ The Constitution stipulates that it is necessary to be a member of the Diet in order to become the Prime Minister.

This is known as a parliamentary system of government. The Prime Minister is voted into power by the members of both houses, and if a majority is not acquired during the first vote, the top two contenders are subject to a decisive re-vote.

④ In the event of the House of Representatives and the House of Councillors nominating different candidates, the issue is settled in a cooperative meeting between both houses. If a decision is not reached even after this, the decision of the House of Representatives takes precedence. In most cases, the leader of the ruling party in the Diet is chosen as Prime Minister (although there are cases in which the Prime Minister can be elected from a minority party that has formed a coalition with the ruling party if the ruling party cannot obtain a majority alone).

⑤ In other words, in order to become the Prime Minister, it is first necessary to become the leader of a political party, and that party must then win the next general election. However, if a Prime Minister in power quits midway through his/her tenure, it is possible for the next Prime Minister to be assigned to the leader of the ruling party without having to go through an election.

任期 / 割り当てられる / 〜を経る

Cabinet
内閣

The Cabinet consists of the Prime Minister and a mandatory number of 18 other ministers.
内閣総理大臣（1名）と大臣（18名）で構成される

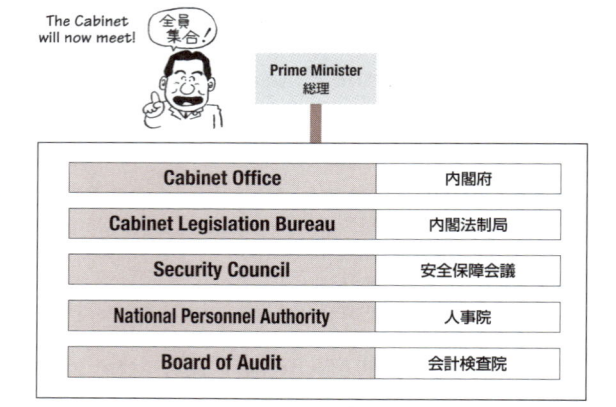

The Cabinet will now meet! / 全員集合！

Prime Minister
総理

Cabinet Office	内閣府
Cabinet Legislation Bureau	内閣法制局
Security Council	安全保障会議
National Personnel Authority	人事院
Board of Audit	会計検査院

Ministries and agencies
各省庁

▶▶▶▶▶

[1] 内閣総理大臣になる

❶ 内閣総理大臣は、一般には首相と呼ばれます。日本の行政の最高責任者、つまり最高の権力者です。事実上、国家のトップといって良い職です。

❷ 日本国憲法では、国権の最高機関は国会だと定めていますので、憲法上は衆議院議長が日本のトップと解釈できますが、現実には国のトップは内閣総理大臣と言って良いでしょう。

❸ さて、内閣総理大臣になるためには、憲法の規定により国会議員である必要があります。これを議院内閣制と呼びます。総理は両院で、議員による投票によって決定しますが、最初の投票で過半数が取れなかった場合、上位2名で決選投票をします。

❹ また、衆院と参院で指名が異なった場合、両院協議会で調整します。それでも結論が出なかった場合は衆議院の決定が優先されます。多くの場合、内閣総理大臣は国会の第一党の党首が選出されます（単独過半数の政党がない連立政権の場合は、少数党から総理が出る場合もあります）。

❺ よって、内閣総理大臣になるためには政党の党首になり、その後の総選挙でその政党が勝利することが必要です。しかし、前総理が辞職した場合、選挙を経ないでも与党の党首に就任すれば総理になることができます。

[2] What is the Cabinet?

① The first job a Prime Minister must tackle after assuming his/her position is to form a cabinet. The cabinet is formed through the appointment of a Chief Cabinet Secretary, who represents the Prime Minister's right-hand man, Ministers of State who will head the various ministries and agencies, and the ministers without portfolio who will not head ministries, etc. The vice-Ministers and parliamentary officials who act as assistants to the Ministers of State are appointed after this.

② There are currently 11 ministries in Japan, including the Ministry of Finance and the Ministry of Foreign Affairs, and each is run by a Minister of State. The number of Ministers of State should be kept within 17, but in Prime Minister Shinzo Abe's second cabinet, there are currently 18 Ministers of State since the Reconstruction Agency was established in addition to the Ministers of State and the ministers without portfolio who run such agencies as the Consumer Affairs Agency. When the Prime Minister is added to this, the cabinet consists of 19 people.

③ In principle, more than half of the members of the cabinet must be members of the Diet under the parliamentary system of government. All Ministers of State must also be civilians. This is known as civilian control.

④ In addition to exercising control over each ministry and agency under the guidance of the Prime Minister, the Ministers of State must also attend cabinet meetings to deliberate and decide upon all state affairs.

⑤ All cabinet decisions are made unanimously, and are officially passed under signature of all cabinet ministers. The cabinet is therefore collectively responsible for all affairs of state, which enables the system of cabinet responsibility to the Diet to be in effect. Ordinary cabinet meetings are held twice per week, and extraordinary meetings may be held for special agendas.

Salary
国会議員の給与

Monthly Salary for Diet Members: 議員月額歳費
1,297,000 yen 129万7000円

Term-end allowance 期末手当
Annual Amount: **5,830,000 yen** (paid biannually) 年額約583万円（2回に分けて支給）

Monthly salary for President 議長月額	**2,182,000 yen** 218万2000円
Monthly salary for Vice-President 副議長月額	**1,593,000 yen** 159万3000円

(As of March 2011 / 2011年3月時点)

▶▶▶▶▶

[2] 内閣とは

❶ 内閣総理大臣に就任して、まず行うことは組閣です。組閣とは首相の片腕である官房長官や、各省庁のトップである国務大臣、また、省庁を持たない特命大臣などを任命し、内閣を成立させることです。その後に、副大臣、政務官といった大臣を補佐する人事を行います。

❷ 現在、日本には財務省や外務省など11の省があり、それぞれに大臣がいます。国務大臣の数は17人以内とされていますが、第二次安倍内閣では、消費者庁などを担当する国務大臣や特命大臣のほか、復興庁が設置されたことで、18名の国務大臣がいます。それに内閣総理大臣を加えて19名で内閣を構成しています。

❸ 議院内閣制の原則として、内閣の過半数は国会議員である必要があります。また、大臣は皆文民でなくてはなりません。これを文民統制（シビリアンコントロール）と呼びます。

❹ 各国務大臣は内閣総理大臣の指示のもと各省庁の行政を統括する他、閣議に出て国政全般について議論し決定していきます。

❺ 閣議決定は全会一致で、全閣僚の署名によって正式決定となります。よって、内閣は国政に連帯して責任を負っており、責任内閣制ということもできます。なお、閣議は定例閣議が週に2回、特別な場合に開かれる臨時閣議があります。

[3] The Job of the Prime Minister

① The Prime Minister is at the peak of administrative power, and the jobs he must perform are wide-ranging and diversified. His most important jobs include selecting the people to form his cabinet and to give policy speeches before the Diet. It is during these that the cabinet's administrative policies are decided upon.

② The Prime Minister must also settle the budget based on his administrative policies, and implement measures that cover all diplomatic and domestic policies. The Prime Minister is invested with the ultimate authority over all ministries and agencies, and is in charge of all affairs of state. He is also the commander in chief of the Self-Defense Forces and the leader of the cabinet in accordance with the principle of civilian control, which was mentioned in the previous section.

③ However, as cabinet responsibility to the Diet is operated under a system of unanimous vote in Japan, all of the Prime Minister's activities must be decided upon by the cabinet.

In other words, not even the Prime Minister can decide everything himself.

④ Although this is criticized for hampering speedy policy-making, the system is also said to be positively acclaimed for preventing the rise of dictators.

⑤ The Prime Minister acts as the representative of the state during diplomatic exchanges. He himself attends all top-level talks and summits, etc., without delegating the Minister of Foreign Affairs, and he also gives speeches before the United Nations as Japan's representative. The people in charge of mobilizing the Self-Defense Forces are also decided by the Prime Minister in principle.

▶▶▶▶▶▶

[3] 内閣総理大臣の仕事

❶ 内閣総理大臣は、行政権力の長ですからその仕事は多岐にわたります。特に重要な仕事は、組閣などの人事と国会での施政演説です。ここで自分の内閣の政治方針を決定します。

❷ その後、施政方針に基づき予算の編成、外交、内政の全てにおいて政策を実行します。内閣総理大臣は、各省庁に対して指揮権を持っており、国政全般を指揮します。また、前項で述べた文民統制の原則により、自衛隊の最高指揮権も内閣総理大臣が持っています。

❸ ただし、日本は全員一致の責任内閣制をとっているため、総理の活動は全て内閣で決定しなくてはなりません。総理と言えども、単独ですべてを決定することはできないのです。

❹ これには、スピーディな政策決定を阻害するという批判もありますが、独裁者を生まないシステムだと積極的に評価されていると言われています。

❺ 内閣総理大臣は外交の場では国家の代表者として行為します。首脳会談、サミットなどは外務大臣ではなく、首相本人が臨みますし、国連で国を代表して演説も行います。また、自衛隊の動員は基本的には内閣総理大臣が決定します。

2 Ministers of State
国務大臣

[1] Japan's Ministries, Bureaus and Agencies

① There are 11 ministries that represent the national organs for enacting all national policies in Japan.

- Ministry of Foreign Affairs, which controls diplomat affairs
- Ministry of Finance, which controls financial affairs
- Ministry of Justice, which controls the protection of human rights and law enforcement
- Ministry of Education, Culture, Sports, Science and Technology, which controls the administration of educational, academic and cultural affairs
- Ministry of Health, Labor and Welfare, which controls social welfare and labor affairs
- Ministry of Agriculture, Forestry and Fisheries, which controls agricultural, forestry and fishery policies

- Ministry of Economy, Trade and Industry, which controls economic policies and corporate affairs
- Ministry of Environment, which controls environmental issues
- Ministry of Land, Infrastructure, Transport and Tourism, which controls the maintenance of national territory and traffic infrastructures
- Ministry of Affairs and Communications, which controls local administration and fire fighting
- Ministry of Defense, which controls national security, including national defense

② In addition to the above ministries, a Cabinet Office under the direct control of the Prime Minister also exists, and this contains executive organs established by state ministers, such as the Financial Services Agency, the Consumer Affairs Agency, and the National Public Safety Commission. Other agencies that do not have a minister also exist, such as the Imperial Household Agency and the Fair Trade Commission, etc., and these come under the direct control of the Cabinet

Office. Also, the Reconstruction Agency headed by a Minister of State was set up as a temporary agency to oversee recovery in the aftermath of the Great Eastern Japan Earthquake.

③ Other organizations include the National Personnel Authority, which is in charge of all civil servants, and the Board of Audit, all of which are basically operated independently.

▶▶▶▶▶

[1] 日本の省庁

❶ 日本には、国政全般を実行する国家機関である11の省があります。
- 外交を司る外務省 ● 財政を司る財務省 ● 人権擁護や法の執行を司る法務省
- 教育や学術文化行政を司る文部科学省 ● 社会福祉や労働環境を司る厚生労働省
- 農林漁業政策を司る農林水産省 ● 経済政策や企業活動を司る経済産業省
- 環境問題を司る環境省 ● 国土の保全や交通インフラ整備を司る国土交通省
- 地方行政や消防を司る総務省 ● 国防など安全保障を司る防衛省

❷ また、省とは別に総理直属の内閣府があり、ここに金融庁や消費者庁、国家公安委員会といった国務大臣を置く役所もあります。大臣はいませんが、宮内庁や公正取引委員会なども内閣府に属しています。また、現在は東日本大震災の復興を司る復興庁が国務大臣をトップに臨時に組織されています。

❸ 独立した組織として、公務員を司る人事院や会計検査院などの組織もありますが、これらは基本的には独立した地位にあります。

[2] The Job of Ministers of State

① All ministries and agencies are headed by a Ministers of State. Ministers of State are appointed to their positions by the Prime Minister. Under normal circumstances, they take top responsibility for everything within the ministry's jurisdiction. To accomplish this, they decide on personnel affairs and the budget as well as propose detailed policies and issue instructions to make sure the ministries are run smoothly.

② Also, Ministers of State are responsible for submitting legislative bills proposed by their ministries before the Diet after cabinet decisions have been taken on them, and they must then stand before the Diet and defend the bills during deliberations. Ministers of State are not only responsible for their own particular ministry; they must also take part in all aspects of national policy as a member of the cabinet.

③ As mentioned earlier, all matters that require decisions in cabinet meetings contain the names of all Ministers of State to guarantee solidarity throughout the party. This means that state ministers are not only responsible for their own ministries, but also for all aspects of national policy.

④There are some Ministers of State who are not assigned to (〜を担当しない) ministries or agencies, but are appointed to special positions (地位、立場) in accordance with (〜に従って) the political issues prevalent (流行っている) at any given (そのときどき) time. The current Abe government has appointed Ministers of State to take charge of such issues as the declining birthrate (出生率の低下), Okinawa and the Northern Territories (北方領土), regulatory reform (規制改革) and the economy and finances. These ministers are assigned (〜の任務を受ける) to come up with (考えだす) policies that transcend (〜を超越する) the jurisdiction of ministries.

▶▶▶▶▶▶

[2] 国務大臣の仕事

❶ 国務大臣は各省庁のトップにあたります。各大臣は内閣総理大臣によって任命されます。通常は各省庁にいて、その省庁の所管事項の最高責任者です。その責務を遂行するために、大臣は各省庁の人事や予算を決めるとともに、具体的な政策を立案、指示し行政の円滑な執行を図ります。

❷ また、省庁立案の法律を責任大臣として閣議決定を経た上で国会に提出し、国会審議の答弁に立ちます。さらに、国務大臣はそうした専門省庁のトップというだけでなく、閣議のメンバーとして国政全般に参与します。

❸ 前に見たように日本では閣議決定は全会一致で行われるため、決定事項には全て国務大臣の署名が記されます。よって、国務大臣は自分の役所の責任だけでなく、国政全般に責任を持っているのです。

❹ 国務大臣の中には省庁に属せず、その時の政治課題に応じて特命の任務にあたる人もいます。現在の安倍内閣では少子化対策担当や沖縄及び北方対策担当、規制改革担当、経済財政政策担当といった国務大臣が任命されています。こうした大臣は省庁の壁を越えて政策の実現にあたります。

3 Modern Political Issues
(Domestic Issues)
現代の政治課題（内政）

[1] Revising the Constitution

① The biggest political issue in recent years is the revision of the Constitution. Japan's Constitution hasn't been amended once since it was enacted after World War II in 1947. The Liberal Democratic Party, which is currently in power, has been calling for revisions to the Constitution since the party was formed (in 1955).

② The focus of the revisions is directed at Article 9. Article 9 renounces war and stipulates that Japan will not maintain armed forces, but the Self-Defense Forces in their present state and the integrity of the Treaty of Mutual Cooperation and Security between the United States and Japan, etc., have long been debated. Those in favor of revising the Constitution claim that the right of collective self-defense should be recognized so that Japan can constitutionally maintain national defense forces. The revisionists also claim that other articles in the Constitution are long on rights but short on obligation, and that it was forced upon Japan by the American armed forces.

③ Supporters of the current Constitution claim that the fact that Japan is a peaceful country is a direct consequence of Article 9, and that it is quite natural for so many rights to be covered as the Constitution is a tool for curbing the power of the state. At the present moment it is difficult to make the required changes to the Constitution owing to Article 96, so steps are being considered to amend this article first of all and the pros and cons are currently under debate.

▶▶▶▶▶▶

[1] 憲法改正問題

❶ 近年の政治問題で一番大きな問題は憲法改正問題です。現在の日本国憲法は第二次世界大戦後の1947年に施行されて以来、一度も改正されずに今に至っています。特に現在与党である自民党は、結党（1955年）以来、憲法改正を主張してきました。

❷ 改正の一番の焦点は、9条問題です。憲法9条は戦争の放棄、軍の不所持を定めていますが、自衛隊の現状や日米安保条約との整合性などが議論されてきました。改正推進派は、憲法上も日本が国防軍を持てるようにして、集団的自衛権も認めるべきだと主張しています。また改正派は他の条項についても日本国憲法は権利が多く、義務が少ない、そもそも米軍から押し付けられた憲法だ、といった主張をしています。

❸ それに対して護憲派は、日本が平和であったのは9条があったからである、憲法はそもそも国家権力を抑制するものだから権利が多いのは当然である、といった主張をしています。また、現在は改正要件を定めた96条が改憲をしにくくしているとして、まず、この条項を改正するというステップが検討されており、この是非の議論が起きています。

[2] Recovery in the Aftermath of the Great Eastern Japan Earthquake

① The earthquake that struck the northeast region of Japan in March 2011 caused enormous damage, and the disaster that followed in the form of an unprecedented tsunami exceeding ten meters in height scored ugly marks across many prefectures in the Tohoku region.

② The number of fatalities and people unaccounted for exceeded 18,000 and approximately 400,000 buildings were damaged, with 300,000 people still living in a state of evacuation as of May 2013. The cost of the damage caused has been calculated at between 16 trillion yen and 25 trillion yen.

③ A large-scale recovery program was started when the Democratic Part of Japan was the ruling party, the Reconstruction Agency was established as a special office, a special budget was made available, and support for recovery started in earnest. However, a large area in Fukushima

Prefecture became a no-entry zone owing to the meltdown accident at the Fukushima Nuclear Plant caused by the earthquake, which caused enormous problems for the agricultural and fisheries industries owing to the spread of radioactive contamination, etc., and this made it difficult to implement a sweeping recovery plan.

④ Many of the villages and communities in the disaster area were already suffering from depopulation before the quake, and as people are failing to return to these communities, there are many villages that face the risk of becoming ghost towns. Owing to all of these issues, comprehensively solving all problems, rebuilding towns with higher levels of safety, and enacting effective anti-disaster measures have all become pressing problems.

▶▶▶▶▶▶

[2] 東日本大震災復興問題

❶ 2011年3月に東日本地区を襲った大震災は、その揺れによる被害も大きかった上に、10メートルを超す未曾有の大津波という大災害で、東北地方を中心に多くの都県にその爪痕を残しました。

❷ その被害は死者、行方不明者は1万8000人を超え、建造物の被害は約40万戸、2013年5月の段階で、避難民が30万人にのぼり、経済的被害は16兆から25兆円と試算される大規模なものでした。

❸ 政府は前民主党政権時代から大規模な復興を計画し、専門の役所として復興庁を組織し、特別な予算を編成して復興支援にあたりました。しかし、この地震によっておこった福島原発のメルトダウン事故で福島県の広い地域が立ち入り禁止になり、近隣の農業漁業はまき散らされた放射性物質などで苦しんでおり、なかなか抜本的な復興ができない現状があります。

❹ 被災地の多くは元々過疎の村落が多く、地域によっては人が戻ってこず、廃村の危機に瀕しているところもあります。こうした様々な問題を総合的に解決するとともに、地震の多い国土であることを再認識した安全な街づくりと有効な震災対策の策定が喫緊の課題となっています。

[3] Economic Recovery

① Although there was a temporary period in which Japan's economy recovered slightly since the bubble economy prevalent at the end of the 20th century burst, the country is still in the grips of a persistent recession. In particular, the global recession started by the Lehman Shock in 2008 and the Great Eastern Japan Earthquake, etc., resulted in a period of serious deflation, and there were no signs of a road back to economic recovery.

② In addition, interest rates were lowered and state coffers went into the red to the tune of more than 1,200 trillion yen. And, the yen continued to appreciate on the currency markets, with no success in establishing effective measures from a governmental point of view being found. It was then that the so-called "Abenomics" policies formulated by the Shinzo Abe cabinet came into being. These policies were basically designed to halt deflation by actively implementing financial stimulus, monetary easing from a different dimension, and growth strategies. Expectations rose in such a way that the yen began to lose value and stock prices began to rise, and it is now said that signs of slight economic recovery are in sight.

③ However, all of these markets are expanding on expectations alone, and more time will be required before a turnaround in household finances can be realized. It therefore appears to be necessary to keep a close eye on the effects of Abenomics for the foreseeable future.

▶▶▶▶▶

[3] 景気回復問題
❶ 日本は20世紀後半のバブル経済崩壊以降、一時的にやや回復した時期もありましたが、一貫して不景気の中にいます。特に2008年のリーマンショックに始まる世界同時不況や東日本大震災の影響など、深刻なデフレ経済が蔓延し、なかなか景気回復の糸口が見えない状況でした。
❷ さらに、金利は下がり切って、財政赤字は1200兆円を超えています。また、為替市場での円高もあいまって、政策的にもなかなか有効な策が見いだせませんでした。そこで登場したのが安倍内閣によるアベノミクス政策です。積極的な財政出動と異次元の金融緩和、成長戦略の策定による、デフレ脱却を基本的な政策として掲げたのです。この政策への期待感から円は下がり、株価は上昇し、現在はやや景気回復の兆しが見えたと言われています。
❸ しかし、これらの相場は全て期待感で膨らんでいるのが現状で、一般家計が好転するまではもう少し時間がかかります。はたしてアベノミクスが有効かどうかはもうしばらく様子を見る必要がありそうです。

[4] Financial Reform

① The long-term recession affecting Japan's economy since the bursting of the bubble economy has resulted in the government's tax revenue becoming sluggish. In addition, fiscal stimulus policies aimed at jump-starting the economy and expanding social security expenditures brought about by the ageing of the population have resulted in the continuation of a situation in which the government's expenditure exceeds revenue.

② This fiscal deficit has been supplemented with the issuance of deficit-covering government bonds, which puts the country in debt. The rate of government bond issuance (including deficit-covering bonds and construction bonds) announced by the National Budget Committee for fiscal 2012 was 49%, reaching 44 trillion yen, which exceeds the 42 trillion yen earned through tax revenue.

③ Also, the accumulated sum of government bonds issued up until now stands at more than 709 trillion yen; an enormous sum that accounts for 17 years' worth of tax revenue and which calculates out at ¥5,540,000 for every person in the country. If the financial obligations to municipalities are added to this, it reaches nearly 1,000 trillion yen.

④ If the state coffers go bankrupt as a direct consequence of this expanding deficit, the economy will spiral out of control and the lifestyles of the populace will be forced into a very tight corner. The only way to eradicate the deficit is to implement financial austerity measures to increase revenue and reduce expenditure, but the effects of increased taxes and reduced spending on the economy will be great, and they are not easy measures to settle on during a recession.

⑤ The ageing of society is also forecast to continue to advance, but reducing social security costs is not a realistic option. The government has decided to increase revenue by raising consumption tax in the meantime, but nobody can predict the size of the increase that is necessary to kick-start the economy.

▶▶▶▶▶▶

[4] 財政再建問題

❶ バブル崩壊以降の日本経済の長期間にわたる不況に伴い、政府の税収は低迷しました。また、その間、景気刺激策としての財政出動や人口構成の高齢化による社会保障費用の増大など、政府の財政は収入を支出が大きく上回る状態が続いてきました。

❷ こうした財政赤字は、国の借金である赤字国債を発行することにより補ってきました。2012年度で国家予算委における国債（赤字、建設を含む）の比率は、49％の44兆円に及び、税収の42兆円を上回っています。

❸ また、累積の国債発行残高は2012年度末で709兆円に上り、これは税収の17年分、国民一人当たり554万円という巨額に及んでいます。これに地方自治体の債務も入れると1,000兆円に近づいています。

❹ このまま財政赤字が膨らみ国家財政が破綻すると、経済は大混乱を起こし国民生活は窮地に立たされます。赤字解消には収入を増やすか支出を減らす緊縮財政しかありませんが、増税や予算削減は経済に与える影響も大きく、不況経済下ではなかなかとりにくい政策です。

❺ また、人口構成の高齢化はさらに進むことが予想され、社会保障費の削減は現実的ではありません。政府はとりあえず消費税を上げることにより収入を増やそうとしていますが、そこでどのくらい増えるかは景気と連動するために未知数です。

[5] Energy

① The issue of Japan's energy has become an extremely important political problem since the devastating accident at the Fukushima No.1 Nuclear Power Plant caused by the Great Eastern Japan Earthquake. The Japanese government has conventionally promoted the construction of nuclear power plants, and selling Japanese systems overseas based on its accumulated technical knowledge in this field was an important political issue.

② The municipalities in which nuclear power plants were located received preferential treatment in the form of massive subsidies, which enabled nuclear power plants to be constructed throughout the country. A total of 55 reactor generators in 18 locations were built all over the country, including the No.1 through No.4 reactors in the Fukushima No.1 Nuclear Power Plant and the Monju Plant in Tsuruga, and an additional three reactors in two locations were on the drawing board. The fact that nuclear power plants do not produce CO_2 emissions is also said to have increased expectations in nuclear power as a measure for preventing global warming.

③ Electricity generated by nuclear power plants accounted for 30% of the national total up until the disaster struck. However, the enormity of the damage caused by the accident has brought to light a system of lax management and cozy relationships between the government and the organizations in charge of geological surveys in the areas of construction and in charge of the nation's nuclear power policies.

④ Also, the main selling-point for nuclear energy was that it is inexpensive, but more and more people are now pointing out that it was not as cheap as we were led to believe. In light of all this, the Democratic Party of Japan—the party in power when the earthquake struck—formulated a series of policies to abandon nuclear power and instead initiated policies that placed the emphasis on solar power generation and other forms of natural energy. However, the world of finances strongly opposed this, and nuclear power is now

back on track for being reinstated now that the Liberal
再び軌道に乗って　　　　復帰する
Democratic Party has retaken power.
　　　　　　　　　　　取り戻した

Structure of a Pressurized Water Reactor
加圧水型原子炉の構造

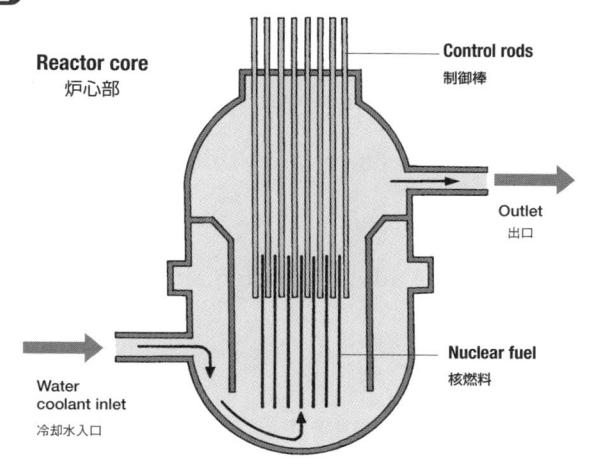

Reactor core　炉心部
Control rods　制御棒
Outlet　出口
Nuclear fuel　核燃料
Water coolant inlet　冷却水入口

▶▶▶▶▶▶

[5] エネルギー問題

❶ 東日本大震災による福島第一原子力発電所の深刻な事故以降、日本のエネルギー問題は重要な政治問題として浮上しました。従来、日本政府は原子力発電所建設を推進し、そこで技術蓄積を行い、海外に日本のシステムを売ることを重要な政治課題としてきました。

❷ 原子力発電所の立地自治体には多額の交付金を出す優遇政策を行い、全国に原子力発電所を建設しました。福島第一の1〜4号機と、敦賀の「もんじゅ」を含めて全国に18ヵ所、55基の発電施設があり、さらに2ヵ所3基が建設、計画中でした。さらに地球温暖化防止に絡んで、CO_2を排出しない原発に期待する声も大きかったと言えます。

❸ 震災前には全発電量に占める原発の割合は30%とされていました。しかし、福島の事故により、事故における被害のあまりの大きさや、ずさんな管理体制、建設ありきの立地調査、原発関連企業と政府の癒着などが明るみに出ました。

❹ さらに、発電コストの安さが売り物であったにもかかわらず、現実にはさほどコストが安くないことを指摘する声も大きくなりました。そこで、震災当時の民主党政権は脱原発を打ち出し、太陽光発電など自然エネルギーを重視する政策をとりました。しかし、これには財界の反発も強く、自民党への政権交代の後、原発復活の路線が敷かれています。

[6] Administrative Reform

① Administrative reform is a political issue that has been demanded since the 1980s. The fundamentals involve the slimming down of the government-run public utilities and huge number of governmental organizations that have been approved en masse to produce a government that is able to administer efficiently. And this coupled with the fiscal deficit has increased a general awareness of the fact that reducing the size of the administration and improving its efficiency are pressing problems.

② In particular, administrative policies based on leaving what can be operated by the private sector to the public sector, such as railroads and the post office, have long been brought into the open, with a wide range of public corporations nationalized, including the division and privatization of Japan National Railways, which was in enormous debt, and the privatization of communications and telephones, tobacco product sales and the post office, etc.

③ However, the bureaucratic system behind the central government agencies that maintain control of the right to issue approval is not easily interfered with, and the general public is increasingly dissatisfied with this situation. The problem of unnecessary public enterprises, etc., has also been raised, and there also seems to be little hope for solving this.

[6] 行政改革問題

❶ 行政改革は、それが叫ばれ始めた1980年代から続く政治課題です。基本は政府主導の公共事業や数多くの許認可などで肥大化した行政組織をスリム化し、効率の良い行政を目指すということです。さらに財政赤字と相まって、行政の縮小、効率化も喫緊の課題として認識されています。

❷ 特に鉄道や郵便事業など、民間でできることは民間に任せるという政策が長年打ち出されており、巨額の赤字があった国鉄は分割民営化され、電信電話、タバコ専売、郵便事業など様々な公営企業が民営化されてきました。

❸ しかし、許認可権を握る中央官庁の官僚制度にはなかなか手が付かず、国民の不満が高まっている状態です。また、無駄な公共事業なども問題として提示されていますが、これもなかなか解決しません。

④ The way in which civil servants handle rights, bureaucracy and other prerogatives is also an issue that can be connected to the overall problem, and one that politicians are hesitant to tackle. On the other hand, there is a school of thought that suggests that too much administrative reform will lower the level of social welfare and other government services.

⑤ Already this is proving to be true, with such adverse effects as the increased cost of national health services and increased costs of state university fees being pointed out. When it comes down to the final conclusion, there is a definite problem when the system allows a few people to abuse their powers through the waste of public money and self-serving rights, and the problem of administrative reform is sure to continue to be an important political issue in the future.

▶▶▶▶▶▶

[6] 行政改革問題　つづき

❹ 様々な利権や官僚をはじめとする公務員の待遇にも直結する問題なので、政治も及び腰です。また、行き過ぎた行政改革は、社会福祉などの行政サービスの低下につながるという議論もあります。

❺ 事実、国民の医療費負担が増えたり、国立大学の学費が値上がりしたといった弊害も指摘されています。いずれにしろ、無駄や利権による一部の人が暴利を得るシステムには問題があり、行政改革は今後も重要な政治課題と言えるでしょう。

[7] Public Works

① The issue of public works is a large political issue. The former ruling party, the Democratic Party of Japan, vowed to eradicate unnecessary public enterprises, and received the support of the electorate because of this. The ruling party announced "Public Enterprise Screening" as a system to restrain public works, which attracted much attention and boosted public interest.

② However, there were certain regions that depended on public works for the local economy, and unable to overcome the resistance from these localities, the world of finance and bureaucracy, the system was eventually allowed to taper out. This was one of the reasons that the general public lost hope in the Democratic Party of Japan.

③ There is no doubt that public works do have a stimulative effect on the economy, and with the Liberal Democratic Party retaking the reigns of the government and the inauguration of Abenomics, a large number of public works have been reinstated as part of the policies to improve the economy. However, meaningless public works do little more than increase the fiscal deficit, and there is also a chance that they allow a few selected people to abuse their rights and get rich, which could lead to other forms of corruption, and there are also many other issues at stake.

④ The way in which the general public looks askance at public works continues unabated, and there is sure to be no change in the way in which deliberations into the problem of running the country in an appropriate manner with regard to public works will continue to be demanded in the future.

▶▶▶▶▶▶

[7] 公共事業問題

❶ 公共事業の問題は重要な政治課題です。前政権であった民主党は無駄な公共事業の一掃を公約し国民の支持を得ました。政権当初は、公共事業の抑制システムとして提示された「事業仕分け」が話題となり、世論も盛り上がりました。

❷ しかし、地方によっては、地域の経済が公共事業に頼って成立しているところもあり、地域や財界、官僚の抵抗に抗しきれず、最終的には尻つぼみになってしまいました。このことが国民の民主党への失望につながりました。

❸ 確かに公共事業は景気刺激につながる一面もあり、自民党政権になり、アベノミクスによる経済浮上政策で様々な公共事業が復活してきています。しかし、無駄な公共事業は財政赤字を助長するとともに、利権によって一部の人への富の集中や、汚職につながる可能性も高く、問題点が多いのも事実です。

❹ 国民の公共事業への厳しいまなざしは相変わらず強く、国のあり方そのものの問題として、適正な公共事業とは何かが今後も議論されることには変わりないと思われます。

[8] Social Welfare

① The issue of public welfare is also an important issue tied into the country's finances. The ageing of society continues to advance in Japan, and the cost of medical services and nursing care in particular are on the increase. The overall cost of fundamental social insurance is increasing.

② There is also a greater awareness of poverty, etc., becoming a huge problem caused by a greater disparity in income levels during the recession. Other social problems arising from this include cases of the illegal receipt of social security payments that are supposed to be paid to people who earn less than the minimum wage, and cases of people dying from starvation because they were unable to receive social security.

③ The fact that people ineligible to receive assistance are able to receive payments while those who are eligible are not indicates a serious problem with welfare policies, and it is no exaggeration to say that it is an extremely big problem. In fact, it is an enormous problem involving the Constitution, which guarantees that "All people shall have the right to maintain the minimum standards of wholesome and cultured living."

④ The conservative movement conventionally led by the Liberal Democratic Party advocates a basic policy of "Self-Help" with regard to social welfare and calls for the substantiation of household lifestyles. On the other hand, the Democratic Party of Japan, the Social Democratic Party and the Japanese Communist Party, etc., advocate a full system of welfare. Whatever the outcome, this is a problem that encroaches on financial resources, and the necessity to subject it to thorough debate is sure to arrive in the near future.

▶▶▶▶▶▶

[8] 社会福祉問題

❶ 社会福祉問題も国の財政問題に直結する重大な問題です。特に近年日本では高齢化が進み、医療や介護に関する費用は増大しています。基礎的な社会保障費用は増大しています。

❷ また、不況における国民の所得格差の増大による貧困問題などが重大な問題として認識されています。その中で、一定の所得額以下の人に支払われる生活保護費に関して、不正受給が発覚したケースや、受給できなくて餓死したケースが出てくるなど、社会的に大きな関心事になりました。

❸ 必要でない人に支払われ、必要な人に行き渡らないことは福祉政策の硬直を示す問題で、重大な問題と言って良いでしょう。憲法によって保障された「最低限の文化的な生活を享受する権利」に関わる重大な問題です。

❹ こうした福祉政策に関しては、従来自民党を中心とする保守陣営は「自助努力」を政策の基本として、家庭生活の充実を求めています。それに対して、民主党や社会民主党、共産党などは手厚い福祉を主張しています。いずれにしろ財源に関わる問題ですので、今後充分な議論が必要になってくるでしょう。

[9] Educational Reform

① This is another problem that has been under debate for many years. In addition to education being at the root of building up the nation, it is also an issue that is extremely close to the hearts of all citizens and has been the target of much deliberation. The issues are diverse, but largely they can be separated into the problem of the basic system of education being separated into a system of 6-3-3-4 years, which was adopted after World War II, the problem of what should be taught in schools, and the problem of the ideal concept of what schools should actually be.

② The system of public education is conventionally based on the principle of equality, but the issue of education suppressing individuality through the use of control-oriented education and rigid curriculums, etc., has been cited. Following this, the "*yutori*" (pressure-free) education system, the creation of schools containing both junior high and high schools, accelerated class systems in certain cases and other

119

systems were adopted. However, the "*yutori*" education system was criticized for lowering academic levels, and debate is currently underway on revising this system once again.

③ The problem of what should be taught in schools is also fraught with many issues, such as the problem of teaching substantial levels of moral education advocated mainly by the Liberal Democratic Party and other conservative powers, and the movement to revise the style of history education that is said to be a "masochistic view of Japanese history," etc. Many different opinions regarding moral education and history education hold sway, and deliberations have been thrown into confusion. The main points of difference center of whether education should be under the control of the government or whether schools should be given a free hand over the education they provide, and there is no doubt that these issues need to be debated seriously in the future.

[9] 教育改革問題

❶ この問題も長年議論されている問題です。教育は国づくりの根本であるとともに、あらゆる国民にとっても非常に身近な問題であるために、大きな議論となっています。大きくは戦後一貫して採られている6-3-3-4制を基本とした教育の枠組みの問題と、そこにおける教育内容に対する問題、学校のあり方の問題など多岐にわたります。

❷ 従来、公教育は平等主義を基本としていましたが、その中で、管理教育や硬直したカリキュラムなどが、個性をつぶす教育として問題提起されました。その後、ゆとり教育や中高一貫学校の創出、一部での飛び級制度などが導入されてきました。しかし、ゆとり教育は学力低下を招いたとして批判され、現在は更に見直しが議論されています。

❸ また、教育内容としては、自民党など保守勢力を中心とする道徳教育の充実の問題や、いわゆる「自虐史観」とされた歴史教育の見直しなど、様々な問題が表面化しています。道徳教育や歴史教育には様々な意見があり、議論は混迷しています。そもそも、国のコントロールで教育を考えていくのか、現場の自由裁量で教育を考えるのかで大きな相違点があり、今後も真剣に議論するべき問題と言えます。

[10] **Electoral System**

① The issue of the electoral system is a fundamental problem that involves the concept of democracy in Japan, and it has also been heavily debated and various modifications made over the course of the years. A large modification was made in 1994, with the introduction of single-seat constituencies for House of Representative elections.

② Prior to this, a multi-seat constituency system was in effect, which enabled several representatives to be elected from a single constituency. However, this system was criticized because running for elections was prohibitively expensive, there were ambiguities in the fact that candidates from the same political parties had to compete against each other, and it facilitated changes in the ruling party, as well as other factors, so the single-seat constituency and proportionally represented multiple-seat constituency system was adopted instead.

③ However, it has also been pointed out that this system has its own adverse effects, such as it being disadvantageous for minority parties, leading to an increase in wasted votes, and results in extreme election results despite only slight disparities in support rates.

④ Another problem that has come to the fore in recent years is the disparity in the value of each vote owing to differences in the populations of metropolitan areas and rural areas. Constituencies with a disparity amounting to two votes have appeared, and the court judged this to be in violation of the Constitution under "equality before the law." This is an enormous problem, and the disparities need to be corrected by urgently amending the division of constituencies. The time for revising the entire electoral system may be here at last.

▶▶▶▶▶▶

[10] 選挙制度問題

❶ 選挙制度の問題は日本の民主主義に関わる根本的な問題で、これも従来から大きく議論され、様々な変更がなされてきました。過去の大きな変更は1994年に行われた衆議院選挙の小選挙区導入です。

❷ それ以前の日本では中選挙区制度により一つの選挙区から複数の代表者を選出していました。しかしこの制度では選挙にお金がかかりすぎることや、同じ選挙区で同一政党の候補が争う矛盾、政権交代が起こりにくいなどの点に批判がなされ、導入されたのが小選挙区比例代表並立制という現在の制度です。

❸ しかし、これに対しては少数政党が不利になり死票が増える、わずかな支持率の差異にも関わらず選挙結果が極端に出てくるなどといった弊害も指摘されています。

❹ また、近年強まっているのが都市部と地方との人口差における一票の格差の問題です。中には格差が2倍以上の選挙区も現れ、裁判で「法の下の平等」に反すると違憲判決が出ています。これは重大な問題で早急に選挙区割りの変更などによる格差の是正が必要です。また、選挙制度そのものを見直す時期が来ているのかもしれません。

[11] TPP

① The TPP issue is an issue that is currently generating important national debate. TPP is an acronym for Trans-Pacific Strategic Economic Partnership Agreement, and it is based on an Economic Partnership Agreement issued by Singapore, Brunei, Chile and New Zealand in 2006. Twelve other countries, including the United States of America, Canada and Mexico, joined the partnership in 2010, and Thailand, the Philippines and other nations have announced that they intend to join. The future intentions of Taiwan and China, etc., are attracting attention at the moment.

② The world of finance led by the Federation of Economic Organizations indicated their intention to join the Agreement and assumed a positive stance toward participation when the Democratic Party of Japan were in power. However, when the government changed hands, one of the conditions for joining the Agreement that the Liberal Democratic Party established as their campaign promise was not accepting "across-the-board abolition of tariffs" as a prerequisite, and the country moved a step closer to taking part when it was confirmed during talks with US President Obama that the abolition of tariffs was not a predetermined condition for participation.

③ Participation in the TPP is expected to bring bountiful profits to the industries involved in the export of automobiles and household appliance, etc., but there are misgivings that it will prove disadvantageous to the agriculture, pharmaceutical, insurance and other industries—with the opposition from agricultural organizations being especially strong—and this will remain a problem into the future.

▶▶▶▶▶

[11] TPP問題
❶ 現在、重大な国民的議論を巻き起こしている問題はTPP問題です。TPPとは「環太平洋戦略的経済連携協定」の略で、2006年にシンガポール、ブルネイ、チリ、ニュージーランドの4ヵ国で発行した経済連携協定を基礎としています。2010年からアメリカ、カナダ、メキシコなど12ヵ国が新たに参加し、タイ、フィリピンなども参加を表明しています。今後は台湾、中国などの動向も注目されています。
❷ 日本では経団連を中心とする財界から参加を指示する声が上がり、民主党政権時代に参加に前向きな態度をとっていました。しかし、政権交代で自民党は選挙公約で参加の条件として「聖域なき関税撤廃」を前提としないことを挙げていましたが、オバマアメリカ大統領との会談で関税撤廃は前提ではないことが確認されたとして参加に向けて一歩踏み出しました。
❸ TPP参加は車や家電など輸出産業には大きな利益をもたらすと期待されていますが、農業、医療、保険などの分野で深刻なデメリットを受けるとの危惧もあり、特に農業団体の反対が強く、今後の課題として残されています。

[12] Territorial Rights

① Territorial right issues have been attracting much attention lately. It is said that Japan is currently involved in three territorial right disputes. The first of these involves the islands of Kunashirito, Etorofuto, Shikotanto and Habomaishoto in the Northern Territories that Japan disputes with Russia. Russia has had effective control over these islands since the end of World War II, but Japan claims them as its own territory.

② The second is the dispute over the Takeshima Islands with South Korea. South Korea has effective control over the islands, but Japan claims that they were not covered by the 1910 agreement between Japan and South Korea and that they belong to Japan.

③ The last is the Senkaku Islands issue disputed with both China and Taiwan. Unlike the other territories, Japan is in effective control of these islands, and China is claiming sovereignty over them. In response to this, Japan is not only claiming sovereignty, it is also opposed to the fact that there is an increasing possibility that China is making territorial claims because of seabed resources in the vicinity of the islands, and claims that China recognized Japan's administrative right to the islands when they were under the administration of the United States in the aftermath of World War II.

▶▶▶▶▶

[12] 領土問題
❶ 昨今、特に注目されているのは領土問題です。日本には現在3ヵ所の領土問題があると指摘されています。一つはロシアと係争する国後島、択捉島、色丹島、歯舞諸島の北方領土問題です。この地域は第二次世界大戦以降ロシアが実効支配をしていますが、日本は固有の領土と主張しています。

❷ 二つ目は韓国と係争する竹島問題です。この島は韓国が実効支配していますが、日本はこの島は1910年の日韓併合とは無関係の日本の固有の領土と主張しています。

❸ もう一点は中国、台湾と係争している尖閣諸島問題です。この地域は他の地域と異なり日本が実効支配をしていますが、中国は自らの固有の領土と主張しています。それに対して日本は固有の領土だと主張する論とともに、中国が領有を主張しだしたのは近海に海底資源がある可能性が高まってきてからである点、そして第二次世界大戦後アメリカの施政権下にあった時に中国はその施政権を認めていた点などで中国の主張に反論しています。

④ The possibility of this territorial dispute leading to open conflict with neighboring countries is high, and it is necessary for all sides to exercise caution. In addition to these territorial issues involving several nations, the issue of Okinotorishima Island also exists. This issue involves the risk of Japanese territory begin submerged under the ocean, and work is currently underway to shore up the levees to make sure the island remains Japanese territory.

▶▶▶▶▶▶

[12] 領土問題　つづき
❹ こうした領土問題は、近隣諸国と紛争に至る危険性が高く、双方共に冷静な態度が求められます。また、こうした複数の国による領土問題の他に、沖ノ鳥島問題があります。こちらは日本の領土が水没する恐れが出てきている問題で、現在護岸工事などで領土保全を図っています。

[13] Abductions

① This is a huge issue involving claims that the Democratic People's Republic of Korea (North Korea) abducted a large number of Japanese nationals in a state-sponsored effort and spirited then away illegally to North Korea in order to put them to work in certain state enterprises. The Japanese government has officially recognized the abduction of seventeen nationals in twelve incidences, but it is thought that the actual number far exceeds this.

② In 2002, then Prime Minister Koizumi visited North Korea and got the North Korean government to officially admit to the abductions, which resulted in Koizumi bringing five abductees home to Japan, and this was thought to be a huge breakthrough in solving the problem at the time. However, North Korea has continued to claim that the other abductees have either died or never existed since then, and no further progress has been made.

③ Japan has initiated various measures under the principle of "talks and pressure" ever since, but the clan dictatorship inherited from North Korea's so-called father of independence, Kim Il-sung, continues today, with the international isolation that the DPK faces growing stronger owing nuclear weapon testing and missile testing, etc., and there is still no sign of the problem ever being solved.

④ This is an enormous problem touching on the basic rights of Japanese citizens and Japan state sovereignty that must be solved. The Japanese government, regardless of changes in the ruling party, is working hard to solve the problem through such initiatives as establishing a special minister without portfolio to handle the abduction issue.

▶▶▶▶▶▶

[13] 拉致問題

❶ この問題は朝鮮民主主義人民共和国（北朝鮮）が国家的に多数の日本国民を非合法に拉致し北朝鮮に連れて帰り、なんらかの国家事業に従事させたという重大な問題です。現在、日本政府は12件17名を拉致被害者として正式に認定していますが、その被害はさらに多いと考えられています。

❷ 2002年当時の小泉首相は、訪朝し北朝鮮政府に拉致を正式に認めさせ、5人が帰国してこの問題の解決に大きく動き出したと思われました。しかしその後、北朝鮮はその他の拉致被害者は死亡もしくは存在していないとの主張を続け、平行線をたどっています。

❸ 日本は北朝鮮と「対話と圧力」の原則の下、様々な働きかけをしていますが、北朝鮮は独立の父と呼ばれる金日成一族の世襲による独裁政権が続いており、核問題やミサイル問題などで国際的孤立を深めている中で、なかなか解決の突破口が見えないのが現実です。

❹ この問題は日本国民の基本的人権と日本の国家主権に関わる大きな問題であり、何としてでも解決しなくてはなりません。日本政府は政権交代の有無にかかわらず拉致問題の特命の大臣を置くなどして解決に務めています。

[14] Military Bases

① The issue of military bases focuses on the Treaty of Mutual Cooperation and Security between the United States and Japan, especially with regard to Okinawa, and it is not simply a regional issue, but a large political issue that affects the entire country. US military bases are located in Misawa, Tachikawa, Yokosuka, Iwakuni and other locations in addition to Okinawa in accordance with the conditions laid down in the Treaty of Mutual Cooperation and Security between the United States and Japan.

② Approximately 75% of the US military bases in Japan are concentrated in Okinawa, and these account for 60% of all American forces in Japan. US military bases also occupy one-fifth of the total land area of the main island of Okinawa, which has an enormous effect.

③ The reason for the US military being concentrated in Okinawa to this extent is owing to the fact that America occupied Okinawa after a fierce battle during World War II,

三沢飛行場
Misawa Air Base

横田飛行場
Yokota Air Base

厚木海軍飛行場
Atsugi Air Base

横須賀海軍施設
Yokosuka Naval Base

岩国飛行場
Iwakuni Base

佐世保基地
Sasebo Naval Base

嘉手納飛行場
Kadena Air Base

普天間飛行場
Futenma Air Base

and the islands remained under the effective control of the US even after Japan's sovereignty was restored through the Treaty of San Francisco until they were returned in 1972.

④ Following this, the people of Okinawa were made to suffer owing to various problems, such as noise from military equipment, aircraft crashes, crime committed by military personnel and the problem of land ownership. In particular, the issue of the Futenma military base is causing the biggest problem. The base is located in the middle of an urban area, and it is thought to be the most dangerous base owing to military aircraft flying low over an elementary school.

⑤ An effective way of solving these problems has yet to be found, and the problem has now been compounded by basing Osprey aircraft, over which safety anxieties still remain, at Futenma.

▶▶▶▶▶▶

[14] 基地問題

❶ 基地問題、特に沖縄における日米安保条約の負担の集中の問題は単なる地方の問題ではなく、日本全体の問題として大きな政治課題となっています。日米安保条約に基づき、日本には沖縄以外でも三沢、立川、横須賀、岩国など方々に米軍基地が存在しています。

❷ 中でも沖縄には米軍基地の約75％が集中しており、日本にいる米兵の60％が駐留していると言われています。さらに沖縄本島の面積の5分の1は米軍基地に占められ、大きな影響を受けています。

❸ こうした沖縄への集中は第二次世界大戦で、アメリカは激戦の末、沖縄を占領し、その後のサンフランシスコ条約における日本の主権回復以降も、1972年の返還まで沖縄はアメリカの施政権下に置かれたことが原因です。

❹ その後、米軍機の騒音や墜落事故、米兵による犯罪、基地の地権問題などで沖縄県民は苦しめられてきました。特に問題とされているのは普天間基地です。ここは市街地の中に基地があり、小学校の校舎すれすれを米軍機が飛んでいる最も危険な基地とされています。

❺ 現在なかなか有効な解決法が見いだせない中で、安全性の懸念が残るオスプレイが普天間に配備されるなど問題が深刻化しています。

Chapter 4
Diplomacy

▶▶▶▶▶▶▶

第4章　外交

1 ▶ The Mechanisms of Diplomacy
外交のしくみ

[1] Diplomats

① Diplomats are active behind the scenes of foreign diplomatic affairs. In addition to carrying out a variety of different jobs in the Ministry of Foreign Affairs, the main task carried out by diplomats is to attend to the embassies of nations with which Japan maintains diplomatic relationships as representatives of Japan and enter into a wide range of negotiations and exchanges with the governments of those nations.

② They are also permanently stationed at the United Nations and other international organizations to advocate Japan's standpoint. Attending international conferences, visiting government representatives in overseas nations and taking care of envoys and leaders from other countries during their visits to Japan also come under the job descriptions of diplomats, and they act as assistants to the Prime Minister and Minister of Foreign Affairs in their jobs, including when they attend ceremonial functions.

③ The official name for diplomats is foreign affairs civil service officers. Nominations for appointments to and dismissals from important positions, such as ambassadors, are made by the cabinet in accordance with applications submitted by the Minister of Foreign Affairs, and they are then authorized by the Emperor.

④ It is necessary to pass the government official employment examination in order to become a diplomat. There used to be a special examination for so-called "career diplomats" who were aiming at becoming ambassadors, etc., known as the Special Type I Diplomatic Civil Service Examination (commonly known as the diplomats examination,) but this has now been unified into the Type I National Civil Service Examination.

⑤ Those seeking to become specialists in the field, or "non-career" diplomats, must pass a special Ministry of Foreign Affairs employee examination to be appointed as diplomats. There are also cases in which ambassadors, etc., are appointed from the private sector, and there are currently defense attaches and medical offices dispatched from the Ministry of Defense in diplomatic establishments located overseas.

▶▶▶▶▶▶

[1] 外交官

❶ 外交の表舞台で活躍するのは外交官です。外交官は外務省の中で、様々な仕事を行うとともに、日本国を代表して日本と国交のある国の大使館に勤務し、その国の政府と様々な交渉や交流を行うのが主な仕事です。

❷ また、国連などの国際機関にも常駐し、日本の立場を主張しています。国際会議や政府関係者の他国への訪問、他国からの使節や国家元首の訪日などの実務も外交官の仕事で、儀礼的な式典も含めて内閣総理大臣や外務大臣の仕事を補佐します。

❸ 外交官は正式には外務公務員と呼びます。大使など重要な職種の任免は、外務大臣の申し出により内閣が行い、天皇が認証します。

❹ 外交官になるためには、国家公務員の採用試験を受けることになります。特に大使などを目指すいわゆる「キャリア外交官」になるには、以前は外交官独特の外務公務員一種試験(いわゆる外交官試験)がありましたが、現在は国家公務員一種試験に統一されています。

❺ また、いわゆる「ノンキャリ」と言われる専門職は、外務省専門職員試験を受験して外交官になります。また、大使などには民間から起用されることもあり、在外公館には防衛省から派遣された防衛駐在官や医官などもいます。

[2] The United Nations

① The United Nations is an international organization created after World War II by the allied powers at that time. Japan, which was defeated in the war, joined in 1956, and Japan's diplomacy has moved ahead since then using the United Nations as the fundamental standard. Japan is an extremely important member of the United Nations, contributing close to 17% of its entire budget, etc.

② The United Nation does not only champion the ideal of peace based on the fact that the League of Nations, created in the aftermath of World War I, was unable to prevent World War II, but also maintains a characteristic of realism. In further detail, only five permanent-member nations of the Security Council have the right of veto to prevent a member nation from being induced to back down on a resolution. Also, the Security Council has the right to enact military sanctions against a nation that threatens world order, and it is empowered with the right to maintain United Nations forces (non-permanent).

③ The United Nations consists of a General Assembly and a Security Council, with all issues related to world peace being debated by the Security Council. The Security Council is made up of 15 member nations, but only five nations—the United States of America, Russia, China, the United Kingdom and France—have the power of veto, with the remaining ten nations being elected once every two years by the General Assembly.

④ Japan has been elected as the governing nation a total of
　　　　　　　　　　　　　　　 理事国
ten times, which is more than any other member nation.
The United Nations also operates a wide variety of specialist
　　　　　　　　　　　　　　　　　　　　　　様々な
organizations, including UNESCO, etc., and the United
　　　　　　　　　　　　　　　　　　　　　　　　　　　　　国連大学
Nations University is located in Japan. Japan is hoping to
become a permanent member of the United Nation's Security
　　　　　　　　　　　　　　　　　　　　　　　　　　　　　　　　　安全保障理事会
Council, but this is not as easy as it may seem.
　　　　　　　　　　　　見かけほど簡単ではない

▶▶▶▶▶

[2] 国連

❶ 国連は第二次世界大戦後に戦勝国である当時の連合国が中心となって作った国際機関です。敗戦国である日本も1956年に加盟し、日本の外交は国連を基軸として進行しています。現在は国連予算の17％弱を日本が拠出するなど、国連にとっても日本は重要な加盟国です。

❷ 国連は第一次世界大戦後にできた国際連盟が、第二次世界大戦を防げなかった反省に基づき、単に平和を理想とするだけでなく、現実主義的な性格を持っています。具体的には大国の脱退を誘発しない様に5大国には安全保障理事会での拒否権を定めています。また、国際秩序を脅かす国に対して軍事的制裁を可能とする、国連軍の保持（臨時）を認めています。

❸ 国連には総会と安全保障理事会があり、特に国際平和に関する問題は、安全保障理事会で討議されます。安全保障理事会は15ヵ国で構成され、拒否権を持つアメリカ、ロシア、中国、イギリス、フランスの5大国は常任理事国となっており、残りの10ヵ国は任期二年で総会にて選出されます。日本は加盟国最多の10回理事国に選出されています。また、国連はユネスコなど様々な専門機関を持ち、日本には国連大学が設置されています。日本は国連での常任理事国入りを目指していますが、なかなか実現しないのが現状です。

[3] Summits and other International Conferences

① There are many other international organizations in addition to the United Nations, and Japan makes a positive effort to join them. One of the most important of these is the Summit (the Group of Eight Summit Meetings,) which is hosted by each member nation alternately every year. The Summit meetings were started in France for the purpose of deliberating on the Oil Shock and the global recession that followed on from it.

② It originally consisted of a group of six nations with strong economic backgrounds; Japan, the United States of America, the United Kingdom, France, West Germany and Italy. After this, Canada joined the group from the second Summit and Russia from the 24th Summit to make a total of eight nations and the EU. As the number of meetings increased, debates were carried out not only on economic issues, but also on political issues, which has continued up until the present.

③ Following on from this, the effects of emerging nations on the global economy became more pronounced, and G20

Summits that involve developing nations, such as South Korea, China and Brazil, are also held independently to the G8 Summits. In addition to these Summits, Japan also attends various other international conferences, including the G20 Finance Ministers and Central Bank Governors meetings and the Conference of Parties of the UN Framework Convention on Climate Change meetings.

④ Japan also takes part in the Six-Party Talks involving Japan, South Korea, North Korea, the United States of America, China and Russia that discuss the South-North Korean issue for the purpose of maintaining security in Asia, during which Japan is able to state its viewpoints.

▶▶▶▶▶

[3] サミットなどの国際会議

❶ 国連の他にも、様々な国際会議があり、日本は積極的に参加しています。その中で最も重要なのは毎年持ち回りで行われるサミット（主要国首脳会議）です。サミットはオイルショックとそれに続く世界不況を討議するためにフランスで始まりました。

❷ 当時は日本、アメリカ、イギリス、フランス、西ドイツ、イタリアの６カ国で経済的色彩の強い会合でした。その後、２回目からカナダが、24回目からロシアが参加し、８カ国とEUで構成されています。会が進むに連れて、経済だけでなく政治問題も討議されており現在に至っています。

❸ その後、世界経済への新興国の影響が強まり、韓国、中国、ブラジルなどの新興国も交えたG20サミットが従来のサミットとは別に開催されています。こうしたサミットとは別に、日本は主要国財務大臣・中央銀行総裁会議や、地球温暖化防止会議など、様々な国際会議に参加しています。

❹ また、身近な安全保障に関する会議として、南北朝鮮問題を討議する日本、韓国、北朝鮮、アメリカ、中国、ロシアによる６カ国会議などにも参加し、日本の主張を述べています。

2 Japan's Diplomatic Issues
日本の外交問題

[1] Japan and America

① Japan's diplomatic affairs were based around the relationship between Japan and the US that was established after World War II. Japan and America have maintained solid and friendly relations in the post-war period, and this is said to have contributed to the stability of the Asia-Pacific region. Despite this, certain clashes of interest still exist on a variety of levels.

② The biggest of these is the trade problem. Trade between the two countries began many years ago with fibers and continued until automobiles, household appliances and other products made in Japan took over the American markets, placing American industries in a severe predicament that resulted in unemployment issues. Also, agricultural products from America's immense farms and ranches were perceived to be a threat to Japan's small-scale agricultural industry, and Japan was reluctant to accept a system of free trade in order to protect its own industry.

③ This is the basis of trade friction between Japan and the US. Another issue is the Open Skies concept for the aeronautical industry, with America seeking free markets in various areas, including industry and services, and with Japan fighting back by raising the hurdles from the viewpoint of protecting its domestic industries.

④ However, the liberalization of trade does not cover every aspect, even in America. The US agricultural industry receives heavy subsidies from the government. In other words, trade friction does not arise from a sense of opposition to the ideals governing liberalization and protection, but from conflicts of national interest.

⑤ Additionally, the issue of US military bases based on the stipulations laid down in the Treaty of Mutual Cooperation and Security between the United States and Japan is also

a huge problem for Japan-US relations. There are critics in
　　　　　　　　　　　　　　　　　　　　　　　　　　批判をする人
Japan who question whether it is wise to follow America's
　　　　　　　　～かどうか疑問を呈する　　　～するのが賢明である
lead in all areas of diplomacy, and this has cast a shadow
　　　～のあらゆる方面で　　　　　　　　　　　～に暗い影を落としている
over Japan's diplomatic efforts. Despite this, Japan-US
　　　　　　　　　　　　　　　　　それでも
relations are expected to continue as the standard for the
　　　　　～すると見込まれる　　　　　　　　　　ここ当分の間
foreseeable future.

▶▶▶▶▶▶

[1] 日米問題

❶ 日本の外交は第二次世界大戦後、日米関係を基軸としてきました。日米は戦後一貫して強い友好関係を維持しており、それがアジア太平洋の安定に寄与しているとも言われています。しかし、様々な局面で利害が対立するという問題も含んでいます。

❷ 一番大きな問題は貿易問題です。古くは繊維に始まり、自動車や家電など、日本の製品がアメリカ市場を席巻し、アメリカの企業は窮地に陥り、失業者問題にも直結しました。また、アメリカの大規模農場で生産される農産物は、日本の小規模農業にとっては脅威で、日本は農業保護の観点から自由貿易に難色を示していました。

❸ ここに日米経済摩擦の根本があります。その他、航空分野のオープンスカイ問題など、アメリカは産業・サービスの様々な点で自由化を求め、日本は国内産業保護の観点から一定のハードルを設けたいという闘いでした。

❹ しかし、アメリカも自国の全てを自由化しているわけではありません。アメリカでは農業に手厚い補助金を支出しています。つまり、この経済対立は自由か保護かという理念対立ではなく、やはり国益のぶつかり合いなのです。

❺ また、日米安保条約に基づく米軍基地の問題も日米関係にとっては大きな問題です。外交全てがアメリカ追従で良いのかという国内の批判もあり、外交に影を落としています。しかし、この先もしばらくは日米関係が日本の基軸であり続けると思われます。

[2] Japan and China

① China is Japan's closest superpower. There are many advantages in both nations maintaining favorable relations. However, discord between Japan and China has been growing wider in recent years.

② China is a socialist state run by the communist party. Owing to the fact that Japan is firmly entrenched in the Western camp of capitalism, it recognized breakaway Taiwan as the Republic of China and did not maintain diplomatic relations with the mainland People's Republic of China.

③ Japan finally recognized the People's Republic of China in 1972 and established diplomatic relations; breaking off relations with Taiwan. The Sino-Japanese relationship included Japan providing development assistance, etc., and a favorable relationship has continued for many years. Japan avoided criticizing China at the time of the Tiananmen Square Incident, which is known as China's most prominent example of suppressing human rights, and this enabled a friendly relationship to continue.

④ However, things began to split at the seam during the anti-Japan demonstrations of 2005. At that time it was the custom of former Prime Minister Koizumi to pay his respects at the Yasukuni Shrine. The remains of World War II A-class criminals are enshrined at Yasukuni Shrine, and China sees this as a problem. It is a historical fact that Japan invaded the Chinese mainland and other nations in Asia, and it was restored to the international community after having expressed remorse for this. Owing to this, the Yasukuni issue is a problem that China cannot turn a blind eye to.

⑤ The relationship between Japan and China cooled rapidly from 2012 owing to the Senkaku Islands issue and anti-Japan demonstrations, etc. Both nations are currently seeking ways to restore their previous relationship against a background marred by the problems of history, territory and other issues.

[2] 日中問題

❶ 中国は日本と最も近い超大国です。良好な日中関係は、日中双方にとって大きなメリットです。しかし、近年日中の軋みが大きくなってきています。

❷ 中国は共産党を中心とする社会主義国家です。日本は西側資本主義陣営に属していたため、当初は台湾に亡命した中華民国を承認し、大陸の中華人民共和国とは国交がありませんでした。

❸ その後1972年に日本は中華人民共和国を承認し、国交を結び、台湾とは断交します。日中関係は日本の開発援助などもあり、良好な関係が長く続きました。中国最大の人権弾圧事件と呼ばれる天安門事件の時も日本はあからさまな中国批判は避け、友好関係を維持してきました。

❹ しかし、それがほころび始めたのが2005年の反日暴動です。この時期、当時の小泉首相が靖国神社を参拝しています。靖国神社には第二次世界大戦でＡ級戦犯とされた人たちも合祀されており、中国はそこを問題にしたのです。日本が中国大陸をはじめとするアジア諸国を侵略したのは歴史的事実であり、日本はその反省に基づき戦後国際社会に復帰しました。その観点から中国にとって靖国問題は看過できない問題だったのです。

❺ 2012年以降、尖閣諸島問題や反日暴動などで、両国の関係は急速に冷え込みました。歴史問題、領土問題という、大きなとげが両国間にある中で、どうやって関係を修復させるか、双方が模索している状態です。

[3] Japan and South Korea #1

① South Korea is Japan's closest partner from both an historical and geographical viewpoint. However, it would be an exaggeration to say that relations were running smoothly in recent years. The basic problems are the history awareness problem and the Takeshima Islands territorial dispute (South Korea views both of these issues as being part of the same issue). It is a historical fact that Japan occupied South Korea and colonized it for a period of 36 years. It is also true that Japan followed a policy of imperialisation during this period, in which it forced South Koreans to speak Japanese, accept Japanese culture and follow Shinto, etc.

② The Japanese government and the Imperial family have apologized for this numerous times. However, there are now increasing levels of discontent with regard to South Korea's repeated calls for apologies, with people wondering how many times Japan has to apologize before South Korea is satisfied.

③ Also, while South Korea criticizes all aspects of colonial
　　　　　～なのに　　　　　　　　～を批判する　～の全ての側面
rule, there are cases in which Japan counter-argues that
　　　　　　　　　　　　　　　　　　　　　～だと反論する
it set up the infrastructure and a system of education.
　　～を整えた
Other issues have also complicated the history issue,
　　　　　　　　　　　　　～を複雑にした
such as the textbook problem and the "comfort women"
problem. South Korea sees the amendment of the wording
　　　　　　　　　　　　　　　　　　修正　　　　　　　言い回し
in history textbooks used in Japanese schools from "invade"
　　　　　　　　　　　　　　　　　　　　　　　　　　　侵略
to "advance" as an issue. South Korea also claims that
　　進出　　　　　　　　　　　　　　　　　　　　主張する
the military comfort women were forced into prostitution by
従軍慰安婦　　　　　　　　　　～を強要された　　　　売春
Japan's military.

▶▶▶▶▶

[3] 日韓問題 1

❶ 韓国は歴史的にも地理的にも最も日本と近いパートナーです。しかし昨今はこの日韓関係がうまくいっているとは言えない状況になっています。問題の根本は、歴史認識問題と竹島領有権問題です（韓国ではこの２つの問題は同じ問題としてとらえています）。日本が韓国を植民地として36年間支配したことは歴史的事実です。この間、日本は日本語、日本文化、神道などの強制を含む韓国人の皇民化政策を行ってきたことも事実です。

❷ これに対して、日本政府や天皇も数回にわたりお詫びを表明してきました。ただ、韓国の度重なる謝罪要求に日本人の中には「何度も永久に詫び続けると言うのか」という不満が高まっていたことも事実です。

❸ また、植民地統治の全てを批判する韓国に対して、日本の中にはインフラや教育を整備したという反論もあります。さらに歴史問題をややこしくしたのは、教科書問題と慰安婦問題です。日本の歴史教科書が検定によって「侵略」という表記を「進出」に書き変えられたということを韓国は問題にしました。従軍慰安婦は日本軍による強制であったと韓国は主張しています。

[4] Japan and South Korea #2

① With regards to the textbook issue, conservatives in Japan believe that the nation should stop displaying a masochistic view of Japanese history, and this has resulted in widespread debate. Heated debate is also apparent over whether the state used its power via the military to force women into prostitution or not in the "comfort women" issue.

② Deliberations into this unfortunate situation affecting relations between Japan and Korea quickly turned it into an issue affecting international relations, and it is currently not easy to continue with the debate in an impassive manner. The government of Japan clarified its standing on these issues with the Kono Statement in 1993, in which then-Chief Cabinet Secretary, Yohei Kono, expressed remorse for the comfort women issue, and with the Murayama Statement of 1995, in which then-Prime Minister, Tomiichi Murayama, apologized for invading Asia, and the government stands by these statements today.

③ However, Prime Minister Shinzo Abe has mentioned that he is considering revising the government's standpoint, despite the fact that these statements remain the official stance, and this has hit a nerve in South Korea. One other point of dispute is the Takeshima Islands issue. Japan has claimed sovereignty over these islands since before the Japan-Korea Annexation Treaty, but South Korea claims that they are South Korean territory and that Japan invaded them prior to the Japan-Korea Annexation Treaty. The islands are currently under the effective control of South Korea.

▶▶▶▶▶

[4] 日韓問題2

❶ 教科書問題は、日本国内の保守系の人たちの間で、「自虐史観」の克服をするべきであるとの意見もあり、様々な議論を呼んでいます。また、慰安婦問題は、そこに軍を中心とする国家権力の強制力があったのか否かで大きな議論になっています。

❷ 日韓関係の不幸は、こうした議論が即、国際関係の問題となるところで、なかなか冷静な議論ができにくい状況になっています。日本政府は過去に1993年当時の河野官房長官による慰安婦問題を反省する河野談話、1995年当時の村山首相によるアジア侵略を反省する村山談話で政府の方針を表明し、現在でもその談話は継承されているとしています。

❸ しかし、安倍現首相は談話を継承するとしながらも見直しを視野に入れた発言をしており、韓国は神経を尖らせています。もう一点、竹島問題について日本は日韓併合以前から日本の領土であると主張していますが、韓国は韓国の固有の領土で、日韓併合に先立ち侵略されたと主張して実効支配しています。

④ The problem escalated when the former South Korean President unexpectedly landed on Takeshima Island, touching a raw nerve in Japan. In the same way as with China, Japan's relations with South Korea contain two large thorns in the shape of the history issue and the territorial issue, and it is necessary for these issues to be debated in a calm and collective fashion.

▶▶▶▶▶

[4] 日韓問題2 つづき

❹ 韓国の前大統領が突然竹島に上陸し、日本側の神経を逆なでした事件から、問題はさらに深刻になりました。中国と同様、日韓にも歴史問題と領土問題という大きなとげがあり、こうした問題を冷静に話し合っていくことが必要になるでしょう。

[5] Japan and Russia

① There has been friction between Japan and Russia (Soviet Union) since before the war. This started many years ago during the Russo-Japanese War, and the issue of deepest contention was that Russia became the communist state of the Soviet Union, which triggered rivalry through ideological standpoints.

② The Soviet Union unilaterally renounced the Soviet–Japanese Neutrality Pact at the end of World War II, which was in effect at that time, and engaged in combat. It is thought that the reasons why Japan harbored ill feelings was owing to the fact that the soldiers taken prisoner of war were afterwards interned in Siberia, where a great many lost their lives, and that Russia invaded the Kurile Islands and the Sakhalin islands after Japan's defeat, over which they claimed sovereignty.

③ In particular, Russia claims that they were morally justified in claiming sovereignty over the Northern Territories owing to the fact that they were the spoils of World War II, but Japan claims that the Soviet Union entered the war illegally in the first place, and that the territory south of Etorofu Island had never once been under the sovereignty of any nation other than Japan.

④ This conflict has gradually been smoothed over since the Gorbachev administration in power at the demise of the Soviet Union up until now, but as even now no peace treaty exists between the two countries, and the territorial dispute has yet to reach closure. However, in 2013 it was suggested that the territorial dispute between two nations has reached a stalemate (and can be solved by dividing the land equally between them,) which has resulted in the possibility of finally solving the problem in one fell swoop. It is necessary to pay close attention to this development in the future.

[5] 日露問題

❶ 日本とロシア（ソ連）は戦前より対立が続いています。古くは日露戦争に遡りますが、特に対立が激しくなったのはロシアが共産主義国家ソ連になり、イデオロギー上の対立が生まれたことによります。

❷ 第二次世界大戦末期に当時有効であった日ソ中立条約をソ連が一方的に破棄し、戦闘が始まりました。その後、捕虜となった将兵をシベリアに抑留し、多くの犠牲者が出たことや、日本の敗戦後に千島列島や樺太に攻め込んで領土を占領したことなどによる日本側の反感が対立の根にあると思われます。

❸ 特に北方領土は、ロシア側は第二次世界大戦の結果による領土変更であると正当性を主張し、日本側はそもそものソ連参戦の違法性と択捉以南の地域は一度も日本以外の国の領土になったことのない固有の領土であると主張しています。

❹ ソ連末期のゴルバチョフ政権時から現在に至って、対立は徐々に緩和されてきましたが、現在も両国間には平和条約もなく、領土問題は解決されていません。しかし、2013年に入って領土問題の引き分け（面積当分による解決）論が出てくるなど、一気に問題が解決する可能性が出てきました。今後も注意して見守る必要があるでしょう。

[6] Diplomacy in Asia

① With the exception of China and South Korea, Japan has basically built up favorable diplomatic relations with other Asian nations. Japan has provided vast amounts of development assistance to the region and has otherwise cooperated in attaining the growth of all nations. A large number of Japanese companies have also set up base in Southeast Asia and South Asia, and in addition to harvesting huge profits, they are also contributing to regional employment and tax revenues.

② Also, now that Myanmar—the dictatorship subject to sanctions under United Nations' rulings—has been democratized and all sanctions lifted, Japan has actively been involved in establishing its diplomatic presence in order to strengthen relations. The regions in Asia will become extremely important to the global economy in the future. Many Japanese companies are now setting up in Thailand, Malaysia, Vietnam and other Asian nations.

③ Expectations for future growth in India are also great. Japan's government is placing great importance on its relationship with India, and huge projects, such as a bullet train system, are currently on the drawing board. The export of nuclear power is also under examination, but this is raising anxieties over domestic energy issues and the fact that India is not a member of the Nuclear Non-Proliferation Treaty, etc.

▶▶▶▶▶▶

[6] アジア地域との外交

❶ 日本と、中国、韓国以外のアジア地域との外交は基本的には良好な関係を築いています。日本はこの地域に多額の開発援助を行い、国の発展に協力してきました。そして多くの日本企業は東南アジアや南アジアに進出し、大きな利益を上げるとともに現地の雇用や税収に貢献しています。

❷ また、独裁政権で国連を中心に制裁を受けていたミャンマーが民主化し、制裁が解けるとともに、日本もミャンマーに対し積極的な外交に出て関係を強化しています。アジア地域は今後の世界経済で最も重要な地域です。タイ、マレーシア、ベトナムなどに日系企業も多く進出しています。

❸ さらにインドは、今後の成長が大きく期待されています。日本政府もインドとの関係は重視しており、新幹線など、大きなプロジェクトも俎上に上がっています。また、原発の輸出なども検討されていますが、これは今後の国内のエネルギー問題やインドは核不拡散条約に未加盟である点など、懸念される点もあります。

[7] Diplomacy in the Middle East

① The Middle East contains many oil-producing countries, and it is an extremely important region from which Japan imports crude oil. However, it is also a region that harbors a great many issues, such as the Iran issue, the Iraq issue, the Israel-Palestine issue and Al Qaida and other international terrorism issues, and the political situation within the region is extremely unstable.

② Japan's stance on the Middle East is basically in alignment with America's. However, the amount of crude oil that Japan imports from the Middle East accounts for a high 81.4% of the total imported as of April 2013, so it is also a region in which Japan and America share different points of interest.

③ There is a possibility that America's system of dealing with the Middle East will have an effect on Japan's interests in the future, and it is necessary for Japan to build up its own diplomatic stance. The entire Middle East is also a region of believers in the Islamic faith. Japanese nationals

are less familiar with the Islamic faith than any other
~にあまりなじみがない
religion. It is therefore necessary for Japan to deepen its
　　　　　　　従って　　　　　　　　　　　　　　　　　　　　～との理解を深める
understanding of Islam in order to strengthen friendly relations with the region.

▶▶▶▶▶

[7] 中東地域との外交

❶ 中東地域は石油産油国が多く、日本の原油輸入においてもっとも重要な地域です。しかし、この地域はイラン問題、イラク問題、イスラエル・パレスチナ問題、アルカイダをはじめとする国際テロリズム問題など、様々な問題が噴出しており、政情が非常に不安定な地域でもあります。

❷ 日本は中東地域に対して、基本的にはアメリカと歩調を合わせた対応を行っています。しかし、日本の中東地域からの原油輸入は2013年4月段階で全輸入量に対して81.4％に上っており、この地域はアメリカとは別に日本の利害に直接的に絡む地域といえます。

❸ 今後、この地域でのアメリカとの協調体制が日本の利害に影響を与えることも考えられますので、日本独自の外交スタンスの再構築が求められています。また、中東地域は全てイスラム教を信仰する地域です。イスラム教は日本人にとって、最もなじみの薄い宗教でもあります。この地域との友好関係を深めるためにも日本人のイスラム教に対する理解も深めていく必要があるでしょう。

[8] Diplomacy in Africa

① Africa is the least developed region of the entire world, and it also has an instable political structure that includes dictatorships, etc. However, Africa has begun to gradually enjoy economic growth in recent years, and this, coupled with the fact that the political situation is stabilizing, is attracting global attention.

② This region is especially abundant in natural resources centered on rare-earth metals, which are necessary for pioneering industries, and the countries in Africa are competing against each other to harvest them. Of particular note recently is the fact that more emphasis is being placed on Africa's diplomatic activities and that the nation most involved in acquiring these resources is China, so Japan needs to boost its levels of diplomacy and resource development to make sure it does not lose out to China.

③ However, economic growth in Africa is a recent development, and it is also a region suffering the world's worst levels of poverty. It is therefore necessary for Japan to concentrate not only on obtaining resources, but also on providing support to eradicate poverty and establish stable and democratic political systems in the region.

④ There are many areas in which Japan could achieve this, such as preventing starvation by providing guidance in the fields of agriculture and irrigation, by providing financial assistance to solve health and hygiene issues, and by providing support for establishing transportation, communication and other forms of infrastructure.

▶▶▶▶▶

[8] アフリカ地域との外交

❶ アフリカは世界の中で最も発展から取り残された地域で、独裁政権など政情も不安定な地域です。しかし、近年少しずつ経済も発展し、政情も安定してきたことで、世界の注目を集めています。

❷ 特にこの地域は先端産業に必要なレアアースを中心とする天然資源も多く、その獲得に向けて各国が競争している状態です。最近特に目立ってアフリカ外交に力を入れ、資源獲得を図っている国は中国で、日本も中国に遅れを取らない様な外交と資源開発が求められています。

❸ ただし、この地域の経済発展はまだ始まったばかりで、現実は世界の最貧困地域でもあります。日本は単に資源獲得だけでなく、この地域の貧困解消や安定した民主的な政治体制を支援していく必要があります。

❹ 農業指導や灌漑指導などによる飢餓対策、医療衛生問題に対する援助、交通通信などのインフラ整備などを通じた支援など、日本が協力できる分野はたくさんあります。

[9] Diplomacy in Europe

① Japan maintains friendly relationships with nearly all nations in Europe. Japan and Europe are geographically in different locations, and there are very few cases in which severe antagonism directly affecting national interests arise, and it is expected that these favorable relationships will be maintained and developed into the future. For all intents and purposes, the relationships between Japan and the nations of Europe could be called "far yet close national relationships."

② There are many nations in Europe, such as the United Kingdom, France, Germany and Italy, that exert an enormous influence on international politics and the global economy, and maintaining close communications with each of these nations and getting involved in all international issues are indispensable elements for Japan if it wants to achieve diplomatic growth based on international cooperation.

③ In order to <u>meet this goal</u>, it is necessary for Japan to
　　　　　　　　目標を達成する
concentrate not only on politics, but also on <u>strengthening</u>
　　　　　　　　　　　　　　　　　　　　　　　　　　相互理解を深める
<u>mutual understanding</u> through cultural exchanges. The
　　　　　　　　　　　　　　　　　　　　文化交流
nations of Europe <u>contain</u> more <u>wealthy people</u> than any
　　　　　　　　　　～を含む　　　　　　　富裕層
other from an economic viewpoint, and Europe itself is one
of the most important markets for Japan when tourism is
included in <u>the equation</u>.
　　　　　　　諸要素

▶▶▶▶▶▶

[9] ヨーロッパ地域との外交

❶ 日本はヨーロッパ地域のほぼ全ての国と深い友好関係を築いています。日本とヨーロッパとは地理的に遠いこともあり、直接的な利害が絡んだ深刻な対立になるケースは少なく、今後もこの友好関係は維持発展できると考えられます。日本とヨーロッパ諸国との関係はまさしく「遠くて近い国」を実践していると言えるでしょう。

❷ また、ヨーロッパにはイギリス、フランス、ドイツ、イタリアなど、国際政治や国際経済に大きな影響を与える大国も多く、日本が国際協調を元に外交発展を成し遂げていくためには、こうした国々と常に密接な連絡を取り合って、様々な国際問題を調整していくことが必要不可欠です。

❸ そのためには政治だけでなく、文化交流も含めた相互理解をさらに深めていく必要があります。経済的にはヨーロッパは世界の中でも富裕層の多い地域でもあり、観光も含めてヨーロッパは日本にとって重要な市場の一つでもあります。

Appendix
Japan's Judicial System

▶▶▶▶▶▶▶

付録　日本の裁判制度

1 Judicial Independence
司法権の独立

① And finally, here is a simple explanation of Japan's judicial system. Japan's Constitution separates administrative powers into three main parts, and judicial power is one of the most important powers, equal in scope to the legislative power invested in the Diet and the executive power invested in the government. Judicial power is an independent power under the principle of the separation of powers, and the Diet and government do not have the right to interfere with it.

② Having said that, it consists of a system in which all powers are able to exercise restraint over each other. The Chief Justice of the Supreme Court is nominated by the cabinet and appointed by the Emperor. Judges are appointed by the cabinet. It is possible for members of the Diet to organize Courts of Impeachment for the purpose of dismissing judges who become involved in scandals.

③ Conversely, judges have the authority to determine the constitutionality of legislation within the Diet, and can examine facts to determine if acts initiated by the cabinet are applicable under the law.

④ Judges of the Supreme Court are subject to popular review by voters during general elections, and they can lose their jobs if the number of votes registered in their favor does not reach a majority.

▶▶▶▶▶▶

❶ 最後に日本の司法制度を簡単に説明します。日本では日本国憲法により三権分立がうたわれており、司法権は、国会である立法権、政府である行政権と並び重要な権力の一つです。三権分立の原則で、司法権は独立しており、国会、政府はこれに介入することはできません。

❷ 介入できないとは言っても、相互に牽制できる仕組みになっています。最高裁判所長官は内閣の指名に基づき、天皇が任命します。判事は内閣が任命します。また、不祥事を起こした裁判官は、国会議員が弾劾裁判所を組織し、罷免することができます。

❸ 逆に裁判所は、国会に対し違憲立法審査権を持ち、内閣の行為が適法かどうかを審査します。

❹ なお、最高裁判所の判事は、総選挙のおりに国民審査を受けることになっていて、投票総数の過半数が罷免であれば、その時点で失職します。

2 Three-Tier Appeal System
三審制

① In principle, Japan's judicial system is a system in which court cases can be heard three times. This is known as the three-tier appeal system. This mechanism is in place under the assumption that a wrongful verdict could be given if a case is tried by only once court, and to guarantee that the verdict has been reached through careful deliberation.

② Under normal circumstances, the initial trials are held in district courts available in all prefectures. If there are any objections with the rulings at this level, it is then possible to have the verdicts reexamined in the high courts located in a total of eight locations—mainly regional metropolitan areas—throughout the country. This is known as the "appeal" process.

③ And, if objections still remain after the high courts have issued their verdicts, it is possible to take cases to the

Supreme Court in Tokyo. This is known as a "final appeal."

④ It is not possible to file for a final appeal unless the verdict given is in violation of the constitution or in contravention of precedents. In other words, the system makes it impossible in principle to file a final appeal based only on dissatisfaction with findings or to request the assessment of a sentence.

▶▶▶▶▶

❶ 日本の裁判制度は、原則として３回審議することになっています。これを三審制と言います。これは１回の裁判だけでは、誤った判断をする可能性があり、慎重に結論を出すための仕組みです。

❷ 通常、最初の審判は、各都道府県に設置された地方裁判所で行います。この判決に不服がある場合は、各地方の中心都市、全国８ヵ所に設置された高等裁判所に判断を仰ぐことができます。これを控訴と言います。

❸ さらに高等裁判所の判決に不服な場合は、東京にある最高裁判所に判断を仰ぎます。これを上告と言います。

❹ 上告は憲法違反、判例違反などの理由がない限り受け付けることはできません。つまり、事実認定に対する不満や量刑に対する不満などで上告することは、原則できないことになっているのです。

3 Becoming a Judge
裁判官になる方法

① In order to become a judge, first of all it is necessary to sit and pass the National Bar Examination. The National Bar Examination is said to be the most difficult of all national examinations.

② The people who pass this exam then have to train for one year in principle as judicial apprentices. Another examination is set after the training, and the people who pass this are qualified as law specialists (judicial officers).

③ Having become a law specialist, it is then possible to become a judge, a public prosecutor or a lawyer, etc. Only about ten percent of all judicial apprentices are actually employed as judges, and it is said to be an extremely tight field to gain entry to.

④ Not all judges who preside over the Supreme Court are

qualified as legal experts. In addition to experienced judges, there are cases in which judges who are not lawyers, public prosecutors or other judicial officers are appointed from the ranks of administrative officials and the diplomatic corps, etc. As judges on the Supreme Court are granted one of the three powers of administration, it is necessary to enable the selection of candidates over a wide range of human resources and not be restricted only to people qualified in the law.

Lawyers
弁護士

Before setting up their own legal practices, lawyers work in law offices for four or five years, during which time they develop a customer base.

弁護士として独立開業するまでは、法律事務所に入って4〜5年実務をし、その間に顧客開拓もしておく

❶ 裁判官になるためにはまず、国家試験である司法試験を受験し、合格する必要があります。この司法試験は日本の国家試験の中では最も難しいとされている試験です。

❷ 合格後は司法修習生となり、原則1年間の研修を行います。そして、修習最後の試験に合格すると法律の専門家としての資格（法曹資格）を得ることができます。

❸ この資格を得ると、裁判官、検察官、弁護士のどれかになることができます。裁判官として採用されるのは全司法修習生の1割程度で、非常に狭き門だと言えます。

❹ 最高裁判事は、必ずしも法律の専門家の資格を持っているとは限りません。裁判官経験者の他、弁護士、検察官といった法曹関係者だけでなく、行政官、外交官などから任命される場合もあります。最高裁は三権の一つの頂点であるため、法律家という枠にとどまらず、幅広い人材を求めているからです。

4 Judicial System Reforms
司法制度改革

① The judicial system has been greatly reformed recently. The most significant of these reforms are the adoption of a lay judge system, and the establishment of law schools.

② The lay judge system is a system in which people from the general public are involved in the verdicts issued during criminal trials. People from the general public are selected at random from the electoral roll to take part in trials together with judges, and they are obliged to not only determine whether the defendant is innocent or guilty, but also take part in deliberations to determine the sentence. The fact that lay judges are involved in sentencing together with judges is the main difference between this system and the jury system, in which members of the general public only determine innocence and guilt.

③ However, problems with involving the general public in

sentencing, such as time burdens and psychological burdens, have also been pointed out.

④ Also, efforts to solve the problems of a lack of qualified judicial officers and the flaws in the Bar Examination (students becoming narrow-minded owing to concentrating only on studying for many years) have resulted in law schools being established. However, problems are also apparent with this, such as the number of people passing the examination being substantially lower than expected despite the schools being flooded with applications, and the quality of those passing the examinations being lower than in the past, etc.

▶▶▶▶▶

❶ 昨今、裁判制度が大きく改革されました。中でも大きな改革は、裁判員制度の導入と法科大学院の設置です。

❷ 裁判員制度とは、一般市民が刑事裁判の判決に関わる制度です。有権者名簿より無作為に選出された一般市民が、裁判官と一緒に審理に参加し、無罪有罪の判断だけでなく量刑についても合議し、判決を出します。裁判官と共に量刑まで判断する点で、市民だけで有罪無罪を判断する陪審員制度とは異なっています。

❸ しかし、一般市民に量刑までさせることによる、時間的、心理的な負担の問題などが指摘されています。

❹ また、法曹資格者の不足や司法試験の弊害（長年受験勉強のみに集中し視野が狭くなるなど）が問題にされた結果、法科大学院が設立されました。しかし、現実には法科大学院が乱立し、合格率が当初予定より大きく下回っていることや、合格者の質が下がっていることなどが問題視されています。

| 全訳・ルビ付き | 英文快読 |
内閣総理大臣への道

2013年9月4日　第1刷発行

著　者　　深山　真
訳　者　　クリストファー・ベルトン

発行者　　浦　晋亮

発行所　　IBCパブリッシング株式会社
　　　　　〒162-0804 東京都新宿区中里町29番3号 菱秀神楽坂ビル9F
　　　　　Tel. 03-3513-4511　Fax. 03-3513-4512
　　　　　www.ibcpub.co.jp

印刷所　　株式会社シナノ

© Makoto Miyama 2013
© IBC Publishing, Inc. 2013

Printed in Japan

落丁本・乱丁本は、小社宛にお送りください。送料小社負担にてお取り替えいたします。
本書の無断複写（コピー）は著作権法上での例外を除き禁じられています。

ISBN978-4-7946-0232-9